I0182062

ISBN: 978-1-945035-12-8

Edited by Black Lyfe Publications

Cover Design by Seoul Designs

Printed in the United States of America

The Demon Within

Cornelius

I'll continue to walk and talk like the world revolves around me and no matter what anyone has to say, as far as I'm concern; it does. I try and I try to let the world see me as calm as I would like it to be but there is just no use, no matter what I think about; the demons think louder, no matter what I talk about; the demons talk louder. I could be in the middle of a sex session with a bad ass woman and yet the demons still find their way into my bedroom.

Maybe I need to invest in a year supply of Xanax. At the very least, when the demons show up I don't have to remember much.

Laying hands on women wasn't my thing until years ago. This woman got slick at the mouth and I lost my fucking mind. She had to have her jaw wired shut for a while. If it's one thing I can't stand, it's a woman who thinks she can talk shit and there'll be no consequences.

I'm not saying what I did is good; but as far as I'm concerned, it ain't bad either. Men in the streets got their women together by knocking them upside the head a few times and when you see that shit on the street, and in your own home as a youngster; the shit becomes your reality. Getting a woman in check is like second nature to me and if you don't want to abide by my fucking rules then bounce.

Every time I look at my main woman Storry, I can't do much but shake my damn head. She thinks I'm a real bull dog. An eight hundred pound gorilla in a glass shop, and she's right. The only thing I know is this. I don't want to be like this. When I think about it, I guess this is how my creator made me. At 6'2, 300 pounds; I'm muscle on top of muscle. I could've never seen myself as a lean tall dude, I need muscle. I need to intimidate people! I need for people to understand that I'm not to be fucked with unless they were damn sure they wanted these problems. Think of a toned Rick Ross and you got me.

Living in Chicago taught me a lot and unless I wanted to be back in jail, it was time I get the fuck out of the Chi. I now reside in Skokie but I play damn hard in the Chi. Don't get me wrong, I will knock a dude on their ass if they get out of pocket, but me living and running the streets has ran its course, and at thirty-one it was time for a change. Hell, I even got tired of the murders, beatings and just all the bullshit that was associated with my lovely city.

So yes, I moved my ass up outta' there. Still close enough where I can hop on the expressway and be on the west side in thirty minutes, depending on traffic but far enough where I don't have to deal with the bullshit on a daily basis.

Cornelius is my name, but for those who know me from back in the day, they call me Corn. I've out grown the robbing, jacking, shoot a nigga real quick Corn that people know me by from back in the day. Not saying if I had to, I wouldn't resort back to my old ways. It's just that right now I've settled on Cornelius, especially when I'm out here doing business with these damn white folks. I'm not racist or anything, I'm just aware that after all these years these motherfuckers still have their foot on our necks.

My life as a business owner has been nothing more than great. I own a luxury car dealership. I have my hand in flipping houses and I own a soul food restaurant. Most would think I was crazy going from being a menace to going all out legit.

All I can say is this, when you have to go to the pen and live on a level four prison yard, it will change some shit about you. Not that I was scared at any time during the time I was locked up. I just knew that was a place that I didn't want to go back to. Sitting in there watching all the foul shit that I could ever see in my life time just let me know I had to paper up when I got out, so I didn't have to go back there.

I never wanted to be the biggest drug dealer, I just knew that having money, however you got it, made shit easier. Especially when it came to these bitches and hoes. Oh, but I'm not mad. I know bitches and hoes, do bitch and hoe shit. So I'm never surprised that I may have to pay a phone bill, buy one of those expensive ass purses that women like or pay rent for one of them. At the end of the day, I made them fuck and suck me. They got a little paper, it was a win-win for both of us as far as I was concerned.

Those kinds of women were exactly the ones I didn't mind fucking with, because I knew what I was getting and they knew what they were getting. It was those pretty, think you owe them something ass women that I couldn't fucking stand. Those women were the ones that I dogged the fuck out of. The ones that I knock their fucking heads off every time they said some slick shit. Yeah, you damn right! I would beat a bitch into submission. You not going to bring your I'm so fine, you gotta jump when I say jump ass around me and think I won't make an example out of you.

I can see those kind of women coming a mile away. I really don't pay them no mind but if they press hard enough, they just may get what they're looking for. Just like Storry's ass. She was one of those, my shit don't stank ass females. It didn't take her long to find out that I'm not the one to be fucked with. She thought just because she was one of those high yella, body right ass females that she could treat a man like he wasn't even a fucking man. She wanted you to wake up and go to bed kissing her ass. Well lets' just say that shit didn't and will never work on me.

The First Time

I was minding my business shopping at Walmart when all I saw was this tall man built like a fucking King. He favored the rapper dude Rick Ross, except he was muscle and better looking. I had to take my shades off and make sure what I was looking at, matched what I saw when I had the shades on. He had on a pair black sneakers. Looks like Air Max from what I could tell, with a pair of Nike sweatpants, tee-shirts and baseball cap. Everything fit his body like it was painted on with just enough room to not look feminine. His cocoa skin was smooth and his beard was on point. Even though I didn't see what he drove I knew it had to be top notch; he just spoke money.

I peeped over at him standing in the pharmacy line; I immediately was turned off, thinking that he must be picking up some type of prescription for something that one of his many women had given him. I watched him while I was in the checkout lane. If it wasn't for him, I would have been pissed off waiting so long. Something told me not to go to this old ghetto ass Walmart with all the others. I had to pick the one on North Ave., knowing I know better. I was here now so I just waited it out.

We left out at the same time and to my surprise, we were parked right next to each other. My little five year old Lexus didn't measure up to his 2017 Benz truck. I got to my car first and within minutes he was at his. We made eye contact and that was my opening to say something.

"Hey, what's good?"

He chuckled a little but showed a perfectly set of pearly whites.

"All good with me. How are you doing pretty lady?"

I knew I started blushing because I felt my face get warm. "I'm good. Thanks for asking and by the way my name is Storry."

I turned to put my bags on the back seat of my car and before I knew it he was standing next to me, and not on the driver side of his car where he was previously at.

"Well, that's a very unique name Storry. I'm Cornelius. Nice to meet you and of all places, the Walmart."

We both laughed and looked back at the Walmart sign. We made small conversation, he gave me his card and asked me to use it when I was ready. I'm not going to lie, I was pumped up knowing that I would see him sooner rather than later.

Three weeks went by and yes we have been sexing each other like crazy. On this particular day at his house which by the way was my first time there, everything just went left and went left fast.

"Where you going sexy?" He asked. "If you're getting something to drink can you bring me some?"

We had just finished another round of awesome sex, I laid there until I couldn't lie there any longer, and I was thirsty as hell.

"Yeah, I'm going to get something to drink but I'm not coming back upstairs. You're going to have to come get it yourself."

I continued to walk down the hall and began to descend the stairs when he yelled out to bring him something to drink. Of course, I ignored him.

Five minutes later he walked into the kitchen and stood in the door way with his boxers on, looking at me like I had two heads.

"Damn Storry, all I did was asked you to bring me a little something to drink. Was that too damn hard for you?"

I continue to scroll through Facebook ignoring him.

Hello, damn are you hearing me?"

I gently laid my phone on top of the black marble counter top. "Look I just gave you some awesome head and pussy, and now you want me to bring you something to drink when you can clearly get it yourself."

I watched him nod his head, suck in air, walk over to the fridge and grab a red bull. I paid him no attention until I felt his hand on back of my head, grabbing me by my hair and attempting to slam my face into the marble counter top. Luckily my hands and phone stopped my head from hitting the counter top full force and doing more damage than it already did.

"Stop! Let me go!" Was all I could scream after getting pulled off the bar stool that I was sitting on. My naked body got pulled and slapped around the house before getting thrown outside on my naked ass. I stood on the stoop crying and knocking on the door begging for my clothes. The only things that got dropped out the window were my car keys and phone. The moment that I got my naked ass inside of my hot ass car, I knew I was dealing with a demon.

Storry

"Damn, Tessa, would you come on? I don't want to miss this damn movie, I'm so sick of watching all new releases on bootleg."

I got so damn tired of waiting on my girl Tessa. If she had a hair out of place then she wasn't going anywhere before she made sure she was Tessa 5.0, as she called being on point. That's my girl, but she would need a whole lot more of something to be on point.

"Girl I'm coming! Please don't rush me, you know I have to be on point before I step foot out of the house."

Tessa wasn't what most would call pretty on the outside. She was midnight dark and wore every color weave or wig that she could find. She had an odd shape like two apples on top of each other. Her face has a permanent scar that ran from the right side of her forehead to the middle of her cheek, just under her eye and to top it all off,

16

she tips the scale at three hundred pounds. Now don't get me wrong I'm a big girl myself, 239 to be exact, but my waist is small. Then comes the round booty and thicker than most thighs. Oh yeah, and I'm cute in the face and it don't hurt that I'm a high yella sistah.

I've been trying to get up with her to see this new movie, Girls Trip and everywhere I went it was sold out. So it was finally showing a week later at the AMC on Cicero and Cermak, I guess after a week everyone has seen it. We took my car since Tessa doesn't have one. As we're riding to the theater, she pulled a half of pint of 1800 out of her purse and poured it into a water bottle.

I just looked at her. If it's one thing I know about her, she won't go nowhere without her drink in her purse.

"Girl you're going to have to roll up these damn windows and turn the air on. What's wrong with? You it's like 90 degrees outside?"

Her ass is always tripping about the heat.

"First off Tessa, it's not that damn hot. Hell, I feel a breeze just riding and it feels good. Secondly, you're over there drinking that shit straight and that's why you're hot."

Only thing I could hear was huffing and puffing in the passenger seat. The traffic was thick and I swear it seem like no one could drive today. Granted it's Friday and folks got money to burn out here in these streets, but I just want to make it to the show in one piece.

We finally found a parking spot. It was far as hell from the door but we were here.

"Dammit Storry, you couldn't find no place closer than this to park?"

I started walking off trying not to pay her any attention.

"Girl you know you hear me."

I heard the car door slam. I just had to turn around to watch her do her normal routine after she gets out of a car. She started looking in the side mirror fixing her burgundy wig with blonde streaks, it was cut in the style of a bob. Then she pulled her shorts from her crotch since they had rode up her thighs while we were riding. Last but not least, she exposed just enough of her breast while keeping her areolas concealed.

"Yes I hear you which I'm not trying to. And another reason you're so hot is you got on black everything, right down to your beauty supply flip flops."

She waved me off like she normally does. I just smiled and shook my head thinking, this woman makes me look good on my bad days.

"Finally some fucking air!" Echoed through the waiting area.

"Two for Girls Trip," I said, to the movie attendant and paid for our tickets. Tessa was already at the concession stand waiting on me.

"Girl, I really thank you for paying for me again but Jacob and Janis daddy is a day late with the check again. I promise I'll pay you back."

"No need, you're my girl. If I got it, you got it."

She smiled and ordered our standard movie snacks. Two large pop corns with extra butter and two large pops; the candy was in our purses. I knew Tessa meant well but she drinks like a fish. She would rather buy liquor instead of food. It's really a shame but whom the fuck am I to judge. I got my own fucking issues or as I like to call them, demons.

"Once you get the snacks I will meet you in theater three."

I ran to the bathroom, went into the last stall, dug deep into my purse and pulled a little zip lock baggie out. I shook it so the contents could settle, dipped my pinky acrylic nail in it and pulled out heaven. Two sniffs into my nostrils and my nail was clear. I flushed the toilet like I had just used it, washed my hands and did a double take in the mirror to make sure my nose was clean.

I walked into the dark ass theater. Of course Tessa ghetto ass was shining her phone light and calling me over to where we were. Smack dead in the middle, fifth row from the back. I heard some bullshit as I was walking but I guarantee no one was going to say shit to our faces. I will say black folks be serious about those credits. I settled into my seat, Tessa handed me all of my goodies and I was ready to settle into this seat and get my laugh on.

Everyone left out of the movie theater about two hours later talking about the movie. Tessa drunk ass was yelling at the screen and shit. I couldn't do shit but let her. I was high and she was drunk but because so many people was talking back to the screen, I didn't say shit.

"You know I'm hungry as fuck. I need to put something on my stomach since I'm doing all this drinking."

Tessa was talking as she got in the car. I was in my own little world trying to figure out if I'm calling it a night after I drop her off or am I going to find a lonely soul to connect with my lonely soul.

"Yeah, we can go get something to eat. How about we go to Fridays or something like that?"

Tessa nodded her head in agreement, I knew she would.

Our bellies were full, my high was wearing off and I needed to get Tessa back to her house so I could get to mine. It's not like we lived far from each other. I just knew

I was ready to go home, shower, change into my booty shorts and tank top, and chill for the rest of the night.

"So you going home right?"

I had to ask Tessa because her ass would be trying to hang out all night long.

"Girl yeah. I gotta release the kids off of my momma before she have a shit fit."

I headed straight down Austin Blvd. coming from the expressway, made a left on Madison and within two minutes, Tessa was home.

It was only a little after ten but I was glad that I lived only fifteen minutes away from Tessa. I stayed closer to Roosevelt and Austin in a big co-way building. My little one bedroom was plenty for me.

At twenty nine I still don't have kids, not even sure if I want them, especially when I see what Tessa goes through with her baby daddy, and then begging her mom to babysit for her. I just think it's way too much if you ask me. I like my freedom and kids don't play a part in my freedom.

I told Tessa ass long ago when she was fucking on Jerald, that's her baby daddy, that he was no fucking good. But she couldn't get over the fact that he was light with hazel eyes and slim. She had already heard in the streets that he was no good and she must've thought that her greasy split was going to make him do a 360 degree turn. I could've proved to her that he wasn't shit but like most women who's gunning for a man, they'll never hear yo; so I left it alone.

I was ready crash as soon as I got in the house. The summer night air was pleasant but I did have my air conditioner on. I watched season nine of Atlanta Housewives until it watched me. I woke up to three missed calls from Tessa, all I could think is, what she could possibly want at ten in the morning? I sure as hell wasn't about to find out until twelve. I turned on Fakebook, still stretched out in my Queen Size bed. I was on Fakebook less than five minutes and saw lie after lie after lie. Right then and there I turned that crap off. Hell, I can listen to lies by turning on the television.

Most people need coffee to help wake them up in the morning, I searched my purse that was on the floor next to my bed and grabbed my piece of heaven. After two snorts I was A-Okay. That was the only breakfast I needed at the moment but I remembered that I needed to run to Walmart before the crowd.

I jumped up, showered and got dressed for a cool 82 degrees today. At least that's what my phone said. I grabbed a pair of red capris with a red V-neck tee-shirt that read knowledge in black letters on the front and grabbed my red and white Air Max.

My shoulder length hair was pulled back into an afro puff. I grabbed my keys and checked myself in the full length mirror by my front door. I was pleased with what I saw and left.

Tessa

I know damn well this girl should be up by now.
I've called her three times and still no answer. She know
damn well I need to do shit like go to the grocery store
every Saturday morning. I heard the television on in the
living room; it was extremely loud so I knew the twins
were finally up and watching cartoons.

They're seven going on seventy. I really wished that
my mom would have taken them to her house last night.
Believe me, I tried calling their day late and a dollar short
ass daddy and I kept getting sent to voicemail.

It's a good chance that he was with another bitch
and didn't want me interrupting his ass. Don't get me
wrong, when he's around he does what he needs to do for
his kids and no I don't want him back. We fucked around a
few times mainly when I was drunk as hell and he was
rolling from popping then damn pills. I looked up a few

months later after we started hanging out just to find out that I was pregnant. I almost didn't know who the father was, but he was the only one I was with consecutively for three months straight.

Once I had informed Jerald that I was pregnant of course he tried to play me. He knew my demon was drinking and whoring around. He had seen me many of nights with random dudes. Once the twins were born he couldn't deny that they were his. All I did was carry them, each of them were a spitting image of him. Even his hateful ass momma came to the hospital with one of his baby pictures to compare. At that moment she knew that these twins were his.

I grabbed my robe and walked into the living room. Thank goodness that section 8 pays the rent because this three bedroom, two bath would not be mine if I had to pay the rent. I get vouchers for furniture and appliances, damn near whatever I want. Watching the kids entertain themselves with cartoons was a blessing.

"Good morning mom." They always said in unison.

I walked over to them while they sat on the carpeted floor eating pop tarts. I kissed them both, walked over to the kitchen which was offset from the living room and made me some coffee; of course with a few shots of Jack Daniels in it.

I felt my phone buzz in the pocket of my robe. I looked down and I almost couldn't believe my eyes, it was the kids' father.

"What's up Jerald?"

I made sure my voice had no enthusiasm in it, none what so ever.

"I called to ask can I come get the kids this weekend. I miss them and I want to spend some quality time with them."

The nerve of this mofo thinking that he can just call and or grab his kids whenever the wind blows.

"Ain't this a bitch, you haven't seen them in two weeks and now you wanna play daddy? You got some fucking nerve."

I stopped drinking the coffee and started drinking from the bottle.

"Hey, first off watch your mouth around my kids and secondly I been working day and night so I can afford a bigger place for my kids so they don't always have to go to my mom's house. I guess if I had of pushed out a baby, I could get section 8 too."

Sometimes I wish he would just drop off the face of the earth. He made me feel like a Queen when he was getting head and sliding in and out of me. Now he acts like he wouldn't fuck with me again if he was paid to.

I remember leaving Lil Keesha party, she lived all the way on the Southside of Chicago right off 60th and Western. She lived there her whole life.

She was named Lil Keesha after her mom. Unfortunately, her mom died giving birth to her. It's rumored that her mom was coked out of her mind when she went into labor. So that left Keesha to live with her aunt. Her aunt raised her but she really didn't care what she did as long as she didn't have the law at her door, get pregnant, or get on drugs.

Once Jerald saw me coming out heading to Storry's car, he stopped me. He asked me questions about what I was about to get into. I was already drunk as fuck and I was done partying for the night. It was two in the morning, so this was the classic case of a booty call moment. We chopped it up for about five minutes then we went and grabbed a room.

Storry tried to talk me out of it but that liquor woke up the sex beast in me and I had been having my eye on Jerald ass. This dude got a room all the way out by O'Hare Airport, talking about the rooms be cheaper out this way. I smacked my lips knowing that was a bunch of bull, especially with all of the surrounding suburbs a lot closer but hey it was his money.

Within minutes after getting the room we were all over each other. My sparkly mini skirt was now on the floor next to his jeans. I was soon bent over the bed, it was on after that. I could feel he wasn't that big but he knew what to do with what he had, and I still was going to need more than this television light to help me get a good look at his dick.

Once that night was done and over with, he seemed to not see me like I knew most people did… big, black and ugly. It was nice to have him call just to see what was up with me. Once I told him I was pregnant, he didn't sound as happy as I would've like him to be but he didn't deny it either; after a few arguments. I went into early labor with my twins. As usual I was at a party, drinking and dancing my ass off until I felt a rush of pain in my lower back and my lower stomach.

I heard people saying, she in labor. I tried to ignore it but the pains were coming too fast. My girl Storry drove me all the way to Mount Sinai Hospital. In a frantic state I begged the nurse to call Jerald. Storry told me he was already on the way. I don't know who told him I was on my way to the hospital but I was glad he was.

Two hours later, I had two beautiful babies both 4lbs 12oz. The doctors let me see them real brief before sending them to NICU. The doctors came in to tell me that their birth weight was low to be full term, even though I dropped them in my eighth month. Most doctors consider that full term because it's a multiple birth. I know it was due to my excessive drinking.

They brought the blue badges down to see me which you may know by their initials, DCFS. I had to agree to get help, by getting into a 30 day program. I didn't want to see my kids go into the system so Jerald did his part by coming to the hospital every day to see the kids. Once my program was over, I was able to reunite with my kids. The state helped me with a place, food and two days a week I had to go take parenting classes over at the community college.

These seven years have been rough but I would do it all over again to make sure my kids have what they need in this world. Guess I better get ready. The man I don't want but do want is on his way, time to make all of us look presentable.

Jerald

It's been seven years and it still shocks me that I have twins by Tessa. In fact, her real name is Teresa. Don't get me wrong, they say pussy don't have a face; but dammit I beg to differ. Like any man looking for a woman that's just as horny as he is after a night of partying, I fucked around and landed on Tessa's ass, LITERALLY.

The only reason I went ahead and smashed other than me being horny as fuck was that she was an easy target, especially after I heard about her through a few acquaintances that described the way she gets down.

I can't lie she's not the most attractive woman. Most people would say that it was her size and that has nothing to do with it. I love women of all sizes, it was the scar that was on the side of her face that fucked up her looks. It was probably a half of inch wide and two inches long and you see all the stitch marks. It reminds me of a long, black, thick caterpillar on her face.

Of course I had women at the time Tessa told me she was pregnant. I tripped on her a little but I knew that I didn't pull out, so the chance of me being her baby daddy was great. I wasn't no more ready to be a father than I was to be anyone's man, I like playing the field. Once the word got out that Tessa was pregnant, the rumors that her baby was mines started.

The women I fucked with didn't look anything like Tessa. I'm 6'2, Tessa got to be all of 5'11, tall as hell for a woman. All around, she was just not my type. I usually date women way shorter. Women I date are lighter and simply well put together.

Heading over Tessa's house I got a phone call from my new chick Shane. She was the only female that I've ever known with a straight up guy's name. She said her mom was so in love with her dad that she named her after him. I answered the call trying to pay attention to traffic and listen to her asking what I was doing. She asked could I come by her house later on so I could take her down one more time. I didn't even hesitate. I answered yes, hung up the phone, parked and walked up to Tessa's apartment.

I had to knocked and ring the bell before she answered the door. See what I mean, games.

"Girl you knew it was me. Why you take so long answering the door?" As usual she ignored me.

"DADDY!" That sound was better than anything I've ever heard. The sound of my kids saying my name with such joy in their hearts; no matter what happens between Tessa and me, she'll never get in the way of me and my kid's relationship.

"Jerald, you here to see the kids not question me about irrelevant things. I'll be in the bedroom while you visit with them."

If I was on some I need to bust a nut right now, I would stay but because my mind is solely on my kids I'm not staying in this house half of the day with her visiting my kids.

"I'm taking them out. We're not staying here."

I knew she would lose her fucking mind mainly because she thinks I'm going to have my kids around another woman. Don't get me wrong, I have a strong weakness for women but I can fight that urge when it comes to my kids.

All Tess did was look at me with daggers in her eyes. I searched in my pockets for a fuck to give and didn't have one.

"Hold on. Let me put them on some decent clothes before you go taking them out in public, around any and everybody."

I waited on the sofa while she and the kids ran around the house in and out of bedrooms looking for this, that and the other.

I scanned around her house, it wasn't that big. It was quaint from where I was sitting. The kitchen was clean except for some bowls the kids had just dropped in the sink. Her furniture was clean, I really couldn't say nothing bad about her place; not that I wanted to. I just wished she got it through her head that we're not going to be nothing more than parents to our children.

I know she wants more but if she thinks I want a whore for a woman she crazy as fuck. I'm not trying to knock her or nothing but hell, that's how I was able to fuck without a condom.

I knew I was drunk beyond measure when I didn't reach in my wallet for protection. I knew I could have been doomed. I later told her ass that if we were going to keep smashing then we were going to have to use protection. Of course she looked at me and went the fuck off because she knew that I knew, she was fucking anyone with a dick and money. Later on I did find out that even though she was out here doing her that she did in fact use condoms. I felt some relief until her ass told me that she was pregnant.

At thirty, I damn sure didn't want no kids. If that was the case I would've had at least seven by now but thanks to abortions, all I had to do was keep my wallet full. These trick ass bitches out here don't give a fuck about shit other than how long a nigga money is and his dick. Once that shit is proven to be long, a man can have virtually anyone he chooses.

"Okay, I think they're all ready to go. I got their bags packed."

I gave her a sour look.

"What the hell you mean a bag packed? These kids are seven, they don't need a fucking bag packed."

I grabbed the kid's hands and proceeded to walk to the door. This chick is crazy.

"Can you have them back here by nine please so I can get them ready for bed on time?"

I was practically out the door when she started speaking to me, I didn't pay it no mind. If I decided to bring them back tonight then fine, if not, then I was going to have to bring them back in the morning.

That's one thing that she knew I didn't tolerate. You won't dictate the time I spent with my kids. It ain't like she was doing anything the next day with them cause if she was she would have said something. That's her way of getting me to come back at night. Now if she can get her fine ass friend Storry to come over then I may come back.

Cornelius

I couldn't believe that I did that to that girl especially after just meeting up with her. I've been working on my anger for year. That's one of the reasons I was no longer with my longtime girlfriend Desi. Lord knows that woman stood by me through all of my bullshit and I cannot lie, I fucked that whole relationship off. I guess you live and you learn. In my case, don't seem like I've learned anything because yet again I'm with Storry and I tried to put her fucking head through my marble counter top.

I want to call her but then again, I could go just fuck with another bitch and forget all about shorty. I'd be lying if I said I didn't want to have anything to do with her again but the truth is she's fun, sexy and my goodness what that girl can do to me during sex is amazing. I've had more than my fair share of lovers but dammit this young woman came in and added some new shit to the mix.

If only I could control my anger. I've been put in jail, been on probation and knocked a baby out of a bitch a time or two. Do I give a fuck? Hell no! What I'm not going to do is keep one of these old ratchet ass broads around, with their slick ass mouth. I tell you, they give you some pussy and lose their fucking minds. I have a business to run and money to make, that's where I need to keep my focus.

Running a Real Estate company is hard work not to mention my others lines of employment but I will say the money big though. When it comes to my Real Estate business, mainly all I do is go to the hood, buy run down ass houses, fix them up to look like they belong in Beverly Hills and sell them. Motherfuckers in the hood would stand back in the cheese line just to have one of my homes. CJ Realtors, is the name of my company. I started this company like many folks in the hood have, I tucked away some street money and built on that. It's just that simple.

Once I was able to buy and sell three homes I moved to Skokie. I continued the business out of my house and then two years ago I found a space for great opportunity. I bought it and turned it into my Real Estate office and yes, that's in the hood too. I want people to be able to get to me, I don't want my folks in the hood to turn their backs on me just because I'm not close enough. So in hindsight, I'm doing this for the hood.

Meeting shorty

I was on my way to the office when I remembered to grab me some Cialis. Now don't get me wrong, ain't shit wrong with my dick but I like to go for hours. Oh and it's nothing that I keep hidden from the women that I fuck with. Once they know and understand my reason for popping a pill they can't seem to get enough. I saw her peeping me. Hell, I was looking at her too.

What I saw was a thicker than most, very attractive looking woman who appeared to be in her twenties. I wasn't trying to holla at that time. Hell, I see many attractive women and I don't go around getting everyone's number.

Like all the others, I wanted to see how tough her game was so I ignored her looks and proceeded out the door. We arrived at our cars at the same damn time. Words were exchanged and then my card. Needless to say she was on the other end of my phone around midnight.

Pulling up in my three bedroom home that's completely empty can sometimes be aggravating. No one wants to live alone but until one of these broads decided to act right, I will forever be alone. I heard my phone ringing that was in my pocket. I waited until I was parked inside my garage before even looking at it. I felt it could only be a woman apologizing for fucking up and wants me to come back or a woman who wants to be fucked. Either way, I'm not interested.

Working twelve hour plus days is where my mind is at. Making money to continue my business growth is what is most important to me. The old me would've been in a rush to see who called and who I can fuck. Just another notch on my belt. Most of these broads see money and try to play immediate wife.

I entered the house through the garage, not even a fucking dog to meet me at the door. I threw my black briefcase on the counter and walked over to my bar that was actually a cart with three shelves. The first shelf housed the glasses and the last two shelves had every top of the line liquor any one man could have. I went for the good old Grey Goose on the rocks.

I walked into my black and brown living room, sat on the plush leather sofa and sunk in. I swirled the ice in my glass and took a long sip. I finally reached for my phone and to my surprise it was shorty from Walmart. Yeah, I can't lie I smiled, thinking about all of that thickness was something to think about.

At a quick glance I really didn't know who the fuck it was. My day was long and I don't know anyone named, Storry. I thought for two seconds and my memory was restored. I clicked on her name, the phone rang five times then went to voicemail. I called again and the same thing happened again. At this point I figured, games.

I took a deep breath and opted to call another female but the more I looked at the time on my phone, 1 a.m. was creeping up on me. All I wanted to do was take a hot shower and relax. My day was long, building permits were delayed and I just wanted to chill. Heading up the stairs to my bedroom my phone started ringing, I looked down and saw shorty name again. I took a deep a breath only because I wasn't in the mood to play any games.

"What's good shorty?" I made sure to sound unfazed that she was calling.

"Well hello to you too. I know it's late but I was thinking about you so I decided to call."

I like a woman who goes after what she wants.

"Well I called you back twice at that, so since I wasn't in the mood to play games I refused leave a message."

I wasn't going to play with this woman.

"Sorry you felt that I was playing games, I got a little busy."

I was sitting on my bed listening to her run her mouth about nothing that I was concerned about.

"You did all that talking and didn't even give a reason on why you didn't answer when I called back. What kind of shit is that?"

I didn't know what to think about this girl but she was about to find out real quick that I don't play games; not now, not ever.

"My reason was, I was busy. Either take it or leave it Mr. Man."

I liked to have lost my fucking mind when I heard her mouth running. The images of me running her head through a brick wall was all I could envision.

"Ms. Lady, I'm very equipped to leave the shit I don't like so with that being said, I'll holla."

I completely was done with her mouth and my thoughts were on the evil side. Fucking her up was what comes natural to me. My demons of fucking bitches up on site has always hunted me. I'm trying to shake off the bad vibes I was having but my mind kept telling me to call her, make a date where she could come over and I split her fucking wig.

I'm not proud of my demons. Dammit I can't shake them. The best thing for me to do is to let shorty go on about her business, before she catch me wrong.

Storry

I couldn't believe what the hell was going on. I had only just met this dude and now we on the phone having an argument; this was totally ridiculous. After the phone went dead all I could think was I need to call my girl Tessa. I know it's late but I need to vent. First, I need just a little pick me up. I reached over on my glass nightstand, pulled out my little zippy of heaven. Two snorts and I was floating.

Fuck it! I'm going to call Tessa. Knowing her ass, she up anyway probably with her ass in the air. I grabbed my phone, scrolled through my call log, touched her name and after two rings she answered the phone. All I could hear in the back ground was loud ass music. "Hello!" Damn, she need she cut that damn music down. "Hello!

"Damn Storry what you doing calling so damn late? Is everything all right? Wait, let me cut this damn music down."

At this point I'm standing in the middle of my floor with my right hand on my hip, swaying side to side waiting for her to get to the phone.

"What up Storry? Girl are you okay?"

Damn she sounded drunk and what not.

"I'm alright. I just had the weirdest conversation with that dude I told you about."

'What dude? Please refresh my memory, I been drinking and what not so yeah refresh please."

This damn girl…ugh!

"The dude I met at Walmart. You gotta remember me telling you about him."

"Okay, I remember now, the dude at the pharmacy. Girl what the hell done happened?"

I was still in awe because I don't even know him like that.

"Girl I can't believe this dude. I can see if we had been seeing each other, smashing each other but this was supposed to be a little phone conversation and that's it. We didn't even get to no other parts of what could potentially be a cool little relationship."

I heard Tessa singing the lyrics to Pattie Labelle's, Somebody Loves You.

"I hear you Storry. I'm just in my own little world thinking about my baby daddy. He got the kids tonight and I'm all alone over here. I'm just having my own personal shit going on over here."

"Don't get me wrong, I could be over here fucking damn near anybody. However, at damn near thirty I'm growing tired of drinking alone and having no one to hold me."

Look at this shit. I call her to vent about some shit that really don't matter then she hit me with this shit. I've always known Tessa to be a strong woman, she don't show emotion at all. I'll have to say that when she does she's indeed hurting.

"Oh shit Tessa, I'm so sorry. You're going through such emotional shit. Is there anything I can do?"

Wow just when you think your shit is messed up, someone else's is.

"Girl, I'll be okay. If I get out of this bottle long enough to go to sleep, I'll actually stop thinking about all of this. I just need to lay down and recover in the morning."

We said our last little words because baby girl was done for. I wished her a goodnight then we hung up.

I walked over to my window and opened my black blinds to peek out and think about whether or not I was going to call the Walmart dude back. It's late and I feel like being petty. Just so I can show his ass that I'm not playing these types of games; well not the ones he thinks. I looked down at my phone, twirled it a few times in my hands while I thought, I decided to send a text first. If he answers, I'd know he's up and then I'll take it from there. Fuck, it's now or never.

Look I don't know what kind of mood you're in. However you seem like you were already bothered before I even called. If you don't want to be bothered it's cool but don't act like an ass in the process.

Storry

Now I'll wait to see if he'll call or text.

The next morning I woke up feeling drowsy. I tossed and turned all night waiting on Cornelius text or call.

Neither happened so I eventually fell asleep. I grabbed my phone which was lying next to me in bed, looked at the time and saw that it was only 6:45 a.m. Hell, that's why I'm still sleepy, it's early as hell. It was my day off so I didn't have to drive them old funky ass buses today nor deal with the people that ride them bitches.

I've been driving CTA buses for five years now and I can't stand this fucking job. I got hired because I knew somebody who knew somebody. I was able to skip all the formalities of the actual hiring process. The killing part is, I'm all the way out here at the Forest Glen Garage. I've been trying hard to get at the Kedzie garage, that's where all my peeps are at. It's a few at the garage I'm at now but it just don't feel the same. I can't run out on lunch and grab me an Italian beef dipped with cheese and hot peppers. Hell, I'm hood and I like hood shit, starting with food.

I laid my ass back down and thought that this is going to be yet another good day. I speak that shit into existence, it helps me get my mind right just in case the foolishness of the day becomes to be too much for me. I propped my head up on my pillow while I stared up at the ceiling.

It was still dark in my room so I was really looking into darkness, thinking about my girl Tessa and how she just went on one about being lonely and what not. I don't think I've ever heard her talk like that and I've been knowing her ass for about ten years now. She always had this no nonsense attitude about life. To hear her sounding so vulnerable was something I wasn't ready to deal with.

Just as I was dozing off I heard my phone beep twice, it was a text. I just knew that it was Tessa's ass, especially since she was up half the night drinking. I grabbed my phone and opened the text.

Good morning, I'm just seeing your text. I'm getting ready to head to the office. Why don't you meet me there if you can? I'll send you the address in the event that you text me back.

I was floored. I just knew that he was going to say something slick. Now all I can think to myself is, should I text him back now or should I wait a few hours. Decisions, decisions. Fuck it! I'm going to meet him there. He wants to meet me, then I say we meet again. I texted Tessa to let her know that I was going to meet Mr. Pharmacy in about an hour just in case his ass flip out and someone like me gets hurt. I hurried to text Cornelius back.

Good morning to you too. I would love to meet with you at your office. About to get dressed now.

I jumped up and got my ass in a hot shower real quick, pulled out a pair of wide legged red pants with a pelum red shirt to match and of course I had my wedges on for sex appeal. Within in thirty minutes I was finished with my shower, had changed clothes, had on my Marc Jacobs' favorite scent Daisy and headed out the door. I wonder what this morning would lead to.

Just as I hopped in my car and started it up I got a phone call. I looked down at the phone that was turned over so I couldn't see who it was. I thought once again that it might be Tessa but I was wrong before. I grabbed my phone and saw Demetrius name across my screen. My body almost started flooding right then and there. The things this man can do to me sexually has set him on a bar all by himself. Why is it that all the best sex dudes are no fucking good?

This man was a kind man, gentle man to me at least, but he wasn't the kind who could do relationships. He told anyone who was trying to be his woman that he wasn't trying to be anyone's man. This man may sound crazy but even though he didn't want a woman, I still felt like in a few ways that I was his woman. Just the way he would call to check up on me to see if I needed anything.

I could call him to vent about another dude and he would listen. Sex, whenever he did come through and lay the pipe down, it wasn't the normal wham, bam thank you ma'am kind of sex that I've had all too frequently.

He cared that I was enjoying myself. He touched me in ways that made me feel I could have melted in his fucking arms. His kisses were gentle. Hell, I even cried a few times due to an overwhelming surge of love that I have for him. I would stop all this powder and partying if just for a real chance with him.

I quickly answered the phone while still sitting in my parked car, smiling the entire time.

"Long time no here from stranger."

I sensed he saw my smile through the phone.

"Long time is right Ms. Storry. You know my phone works as well. The number is still the same?"

I knew where he was going with this.

"I understand all of that. However, I've explained to you a thousand times why I don't call."

I felt some anger coming over me at that moment. I had to take a few deep breaths to calm down.

"Please explain those reasons again, because if they are the same ones you been telling me about, then like I said then, your reasons isn't strong enough to with stand a fucking tornado."

"Like I've said before, you know how much love I have for you and I never want to call you and my call gets ignored because you're with another bitch."

"Are you referring to yourself as a bitch?"

"No, I said another bitch."

"By using the word another you're stating you're one, as well as the other woman I may be with at the time of your call."

Demetrius got on my fucking nerves with all the technical shit.

"Why do you have to be so damn technical all the damn time?"

"Because when you speak, I want you to be more aware of what you're saying. That's all."

Our banter went on for about ten more minutes before I heard the magic words. He asked could he come over and said that he missed me. Before my brain could respond properly my body said yes all ready. Which was followed with a verbal yes.

"How long will it be before you can get here?" I was already exiting my car and heading back inside of my apartment.

"Give me and hour. I have to shower and get dressed first." I was taking clothes off at the door just to take another shower and prep all over again.

"I'll see you then."

We disconnected the call. I was so excited to have this man in my presence again that when I do see him, it always seems unreal.

Demetrius

I knew all I had to do was call and little Ms. Storry was going to answer. One thing for sure and two for certain, that woman's crazy about me. I could have her wrapped around my pinky finger way more than she is right now. I wouldn't dare play on her heart strings like that. That's the reason I stay away months at a time, give our last encounter time to become a distant memory.

That woman would be the one if it wasn't for my desire to not settle down. She always thinking that I'm with multiple women. I know she can't understand that a man like myself don't want to be tied down. I just want to sleep with different women.

I didn't want to call her but two months had already passed and when I saw her standing in the Walmart parking lot talking to a guy I know from the neighborhood, I assumed that she was involved; it's not like it would've made a difference. Based on how she feels about me she would drop anyone she's currently with but like I said, I won't play on that until it's something that I want.

Storry left a mark on me after meeting that woman three years ago at the Blue Note Jazz Club. I was on my second bottle of Remy when I saw her at the bar trying to get the bartender's attention and like usual up in here; nothing. I waved my hand and since I'm really good friends with the bartender. I was immediately noticed. I put a bug in the bartender's ear about shorty that was trying to get her attention.

I told the bartender to give her whatever she wanted.

"Instead of a glass give her a bottle."

I saw the bartender hand her a bottle of Remy. That made me smile just knowing we drink the same thing.

She noticed me as I walked over and said, "Thank you".

Yeah she shimmied her way back to the dance floor holding her bottle up in the air. She was on the dance floor with some other girls grinding all on each other. I smiled, lifted my bottle and returned to my boys.

I knew that night that I would have her anyway that I wanted. What I didn't know is that she would reign in my thoughts just as I would in hers. Shit, last thing I remembered was her and I in my truck heading to the expressway on the way to the west side of Chicago.

The heat was crucial that night so I had the air conditioner on in the truck. She was getting frisky like she hadn't been with a man in a while. I knew it was the liquor talking but I was all up for whatever it had to say.

It was two in the morning. I looked over at her every chance I got since I was driving. The glimpse I was getting from her thighs, her breast and her neck, she was a beautiful sister. I also sensed that she was drunker than she should've been. Her bottle of Remy, well half bottle of Remy was sitting in the back on the floor. I guess she can't hold her liquor. Just as I was focusing back on the road she caught me starring at her.

"What are you looking at?"

I didn't do nothing but smile. "Your fine ass."

Nothing else was said until I pulled up on my block. I parked, staggered over to the passenger side of the truck and assisted Storry out. I put my hand on the small of her back and walked her to my apartment. At two in the morning the block was still engaging with friends and neighbors.

"Hey, Demetrius."

I saw Yollanda walking up to me. I couldn't get Storry in the house fast enough.

She must have sensed something because I was trying to keep it moving and Storry feet was planted like cement.

"Hey, Demetrius. What you not speaking today?"

I didn't have time for this shit.

"What's good Yollanda?"

She was shooting daggers as if I gave a fuck.

"You tell me, you the one creeping at two in the morning and then don't even have the common decency to introduce your little friend."

I laughed and pushed Storry's ass up the stairs and into the house as fast as I could.

Once inside the apartment I cut on the lights and some music from my phone and offered Storry a seat. She sat on the sofa, laid her head back and took a deep breath. I watched her every move.

"Before this goes any further, do you care to explain who the fuck ol' girl was?"

I knew this shit was coming. I leaned up against the wall that was directly in front of her so she could see my body language and face regarding this woman.

"Yes she and I have had sex, wasn't nothing more. She cool people, yet messy.

Like everyone else I told her I didn't want a relationship and she couldn't handle it, so I stopped fucking with her all together and that's where we're at with it. I can be cordial but nothing else."

I don't know what she was looking for. However, she watched me with uncertainty.

"Are you sure? I don't want to get caught up in anything because of a smash buddy."

I took a deep breath.

"She's not a smash buddy. That would mean I'm still smashing but she did get smashed a few times just like whomever else I decided to smash. Trust me, she ain't special like that."

All I wanted was for this conversation to end so we could get down to what we came here for. I didn't want any problems at this moment, I just wanted her.

"Well enough about her and anyone else for that matter, I simply want to be with you. I didn't come to your home to talk about past booty. I just want to give you some new booty."

We both laughed at her statement.

"Oh yeah. You want to give me some new booty huh? Well since we both want to do what you want to do then how about we walk into my bathroom, take a hot shower together, then see what happens."

Storry stood from the sofa and kissed me with such passion. It wasn't one of those drunken kisses but one of those I love you kind of kisses.

We walked into the bathroom. I reached over turned the cold metal knobs and watch the bathroom fill up with steam in mere seconds.

"You want me to undress you?"

I was in a hurry to get her clothes off. I just didn't want to seem anxious.

"No, we can watch each other take off our own clothes though."

My thoughts were all over the place. I've never had a woman say that shit, they have all wanted me to take their clothes off for them.

My surround speakers throughout my apartment made the music crisp and clear even though we were in the bathroom. She didn't do a sultry dance while taking off her clothes but when she took them off, she was looking damn sexy too me. Those big yellow legs exposed, even her stomach was sexy. She didn't have kids that I knew of, but her stretch marks was there and ready to be kissed. Her breast were full, not too much but just big enough for my big hands.

I watched her step into the shower. There were already clean towels in the shower that I had put in there earlier, knowing this could turn out to be the kind of night that I needed to supply clean towels. I stepped in right behind her. The shower was average. The shower head sprayed out like a water fall. I grabbed the Dove out of the window seal, squeezed some in the palm of my hand, made circular motions on her back then found my way to her supple breast, she let out a soft moan while her hands rested on the shower wall in front of her.

My movements found its way to her neck, massaging her upper body with soapy hands until she lifted her left leg and rested it on the rim of the bathtub. I poured more soap in my hands this time. I started with her waist and just like her breast, her ass was just as full.

I traced the crack of her ass until I was touching the treasure that she was willing to let me have. I made slow strokes back and forth. I saw the arch in her lower back get deeper. She turned and looked at me, grabbed the soap and mimicked what I had done to her. I was already to go when she grabbed my dick and stroked it just as gentle and soft as I had did her. She didn't blink or take her eyes off of me. I tried to control myself. I let out a moan or two my damn self before she stopped and let the now warm water rinse me off.

I helped her out, then I followed behind. I grabbed her a towel knowing that even though it's hot in here, it would be cool once she opened the door do to the central air. She wrapped the towel around her as best as she could.

"No need to worry about covering up, that towel is coming off."

I dried off just enough so the cool air wouldn't shock my body. We walked out down the small hall and to the left was the kitchen and my bedroom. Damn glad I don't keep a nasty ass house.

I guess she sensed that the bedroom was this way I followed like it was her house, she stopped short when she came to the bedroom.

"What's wrong Storry?"

I didn't know what her problem was.

"Um do you have kids and I didn't know you had two bedrooms."

I looked over at the second bedroom that was right next to mine, the door was open.

"You just got here. You couldn't have known much of nothing of my apartment. Sometimes my sister comes to town and my niece and nephew sleep in there while she go chasing some random out here in the streets."

I hope she was sold on my story because I didn't have time to argue with her about anything that didn't matter. She continued to make her way to my bedroom, I closed the door behind me and flicked the light switch on. Gray and black sheets and a comforter dressed the king size bed. A gray and black mirrored, six drawer dresser sat directly across from my bed with a 55' inch flat screen mounted on the wall with cable of course.

"Damn, I'm impressed. You have a beautiful room here."

Two black high back leather chairs sat in opposite corners of the bed, the room was nice. I'm glad she eased up.

"Hell yeah, I don't need everybody that come through here sitting on my bed."

Storry turned and looked at me with a smile.

"Can I sit on your bed?"

I gave her a very nonchalant look.

"Girl you can sit, lay, sleep and cum in my bed."

After my last word she dropped her towel that wasn't doing a very good job covering her up anyway.

"Well then come get some of this new booty."

Finally I was about to fuck her whole understanding up.

Tessa

Now I don't know what has gotten into me. I never swooned over a guy, especially a guy who tries to act like I ain't shit, even when I'm the mother of his kids. Don't get me wrong, Jerald is handsome, thin frame, curly hair and light with hazel eyes. He got that mix thang going on. I hate seeing him come just as much as I hated seeing him go but a few one night stands led to a pregnancy and boom, twins.

I should let him keep them for good so he can see how this shit ain't no joke raising kids, especially two of them. If I wasn't so worried about section 8 taking my voucher because I didn't have my kids, I would tell him to keep them and I would disappear. Not saying that I don't love my kids because God knows I do, however a bitch like me need a fucking break.

I gotta lay off this damn liquor. I remember Storry calling me last night but the only thing I did was talk about how sorry I was feeling for myself. I don't talk like that, the liquor was speaking for me which I don't need. At twenty-eight I want someone to call my own but there's no way in hell I'm gonna cry about it. I can get dick anytime I want. Far as I'm concerned that's all these dudes are good for anyway. Bring me a big stiff one and then move the fuck around. I don't want no drama or bullshit, I create enough of that shit on my own.

Since it's Sunday maybe I'll try to catch up on my reality shows and cook. I just went to the grocery store yesterday, the cabinets and fridge are over flowing. The kids will be back today so it'll be nice to have a hot meal waiting on them when they arrive and if I know Storry she'll be dropping by and be ready to get her grub on. If I don't know nothing else, I know how to jam in the kitchen, thanks to my momma.

I hopped off the same kitchen stool I sit at when I'm watching the kids play, or if they're watching T.V.

I searched the cabinets for dinner. I quickly decided to cook some smothered chicken with gravy and onions, garlic butter mashed potatoes and parmesan corn on the cob. To wash it all down I made a pitcher of homemade lemonade, where you have to roll the lemons by hand to soften them up.

I felt good about today even though my kids weren't home yet. I just want today to become a great start to a lot of new beginnings for me and my kids. I know Jerald's not coming back to me the way I want him to even though if he wanted some ass he would surely get it.

I walked around my house with some lounge pants on and a tank top. The sun was shining bright so I opened the curtains and blinds. The central air was blowing on low so the apartment was at a feel good temperature.

I heard some commotion outside, I didn't want to be nosey. I looked at the time and it was only ten in the morning. I stepped outside and once again I saw Jazz which is my next door neighbor screaming down on her so called man.

He must have come in yet again after the sun instead of the other way around.

"Damn, Chris, every fucking time you do this shit you say you're going to change and the same old shit!"

I saw Chris not really paying her any attention. He was actually trying to walk around her and go in the house.

"Look, Jazz, I was at the studio all fucking night long. I'm tired and I don't have time for this shit! Can we please go in the house, unless you like showing out for these folks out here?"

I even started too laughed when they both noticed me standing in front of the house looking in their direction.

"Fuck these folks out here! They don't live with us and I'm not fucking them. Therefore they're not my concern, you are. I'm sick of going through this shit with you!"

Damn, all that woman did was scream down on him. Now what she should've been doing is taking him in the house so he could get some head to keep him calm. But instead she want to try and make a point by letting the whole damn block know their business.

At this time of the morning especially in the summer time all sorts of people were outside just getting there morning started and she want to be out here looking like a fucking fool. I took my ass back in the house grabbed my phone off the kitchen counter and texted Chris.

Just letting him know he can come over to get some relaxation. He texted me right back, letting me know he will be over shortly and to keep the back door open. They didn't make that song, The Clean-up Woman for nothing, these bitches better recognize.

I'm doing her ass a favor. I'm going to get him right then he'll be back over there with sweet kisses for her and she'll calm her ass down like always.

Chris is a cool dude and his sex game is all that. However, he's a whore if he fucking me and I live right next door to them. I know damn well he fucking a whole lot more women. I don't need all that stress that he seem to bring into women lives.

I'm trying to de-stress. I got enough on my plate wondering about a baby daddy who I'm not with, then trying to get my head right is another challenge and now I have this dude next door who I can have anytime but he stuck on Ms. Big Booty next door.

I started getting my dinner ready for tonight so when the kids came home dinner would be out the way.

Fifteen minutes later I heard my back door open. I made sure I changed real quick into some booty shorts that were pulled a little higher than normal. It really didn't matter because I had ass for days. I had a pink tank top on that was virtually see through. I made sure my nipples where ready to cut glass, by giving them a little pinch and tug. By the time he reached me I was still standing there with chicken in my hand.

"Sorry you had to see that shit Tessa."

I gave him a confused look because I really don't care what they go through.

"Chris you know I could care less about what you two go through. I've never wanted to know anything about your relationship but you always offer so I listen."

He went to sit on the sofa.

"Yeah I know but we've been sleeping with each other for a year. I figure at the very least I can talk to you from time to time."

I know damn well this dude is not getting mushy on me.

"Chris, we good. That's what I'm here for. I know you're in an unhappy situation. I'm just glad that I can take the pain away."

I walked in front of him and didn't say a word. I made my booty clap and jiggle knowing that he was enjoying the show.

"Damn girl, you're something else."

I looked back at him over my right shoulder.

"Yeah I know."

Once he stood up he wrapped his left arm around my waist and walked me the few steps to the sofa. I was on my knees facing the back of the couch. I felt my shorts being pulled down so I made sure to keep my ass wiggling. There was a pause so I looked back and saw that he was taking off all his clothes.

This was normal but he did need to hurry up.

"Damn girl, I been needing some of you."

I didn't say a word I was already wet and ready to go.

"Take your shirt off. I want to be able to grab those beautiful ass breast of yours."

I did as I was told. I felt Chris trail the crack of my ass with his third leg. Next thing I know he was enjoying the inside of me just as much as I was enjoying him. It wasn't a part of my body that he didn't touch, he was very attentive and attractive. I just wanted and needed him at the moment. He made me feel good, I made him feel good and yet when this was over he'll be back next door like this didn't even happen. So I live in this moment and enjoyed him for the next thirty minutes.

When he collapsed on top of my back I knew he was done and so was I. I climaxed three times. Boy I tell you this man was good for my body. He peeled himself off of me and I walked to the bathroom without my clothes on, he followed close behind.

"If only you wasn't sleeping with so many damn men I could see myself being with you."

I stopped dead in my tracks. I knew damn well he wasn't on this shit again; I spoke without even looking at him.

"Don't start this again Chris. From the moment you started sleeping with me and you had a whole woman next door, I knew that we could never be. I know I'm just as wrong in this as you are and for that reason this is all we could ever be to one another, sex buddies."

I continued to walk in the bathroom with him still following behind. I hopped in the shower while he washed his dick off in the sink. Before I got out the shower he was gone and my back door was locked.

Shane

I can't believe I called Jerald ass a day or two ago and I still haven't heard from him. Now granted I know he has kids but don't leave me hanging because as soon as I do it to him he'll have a fucking problem. I usually don't mess around with guys who have kids. However, there's a very slim chance of meeting someone that doesn't have any.

I just had to reshape my way of thinking in hopes that I don't run across a man with a fucked up baby momma. I don't have no kids and don't want no kids. No woman has to ever worry about me trying to play momma to her kids.

Like most men I meet, I met Jerald going into the hole in the wall restaurant after hours where the food was greasy and helped soak up some of that damn liquor so you wouldn't be calling earl later on. I was with my girls and he was with a group of men and women. I saw one woman holding on to him for dear life so I paid it no mind, until he walked over to my table, asked me my name and wanted to know could we switch numbers. I peeped the chubby chick that was previously all over him looking in our direction, then back to a meaningless conversation with the other people that sat at her table.

I smiled, grabbed his phone and programmed my number in it. With a wink of his eye he left to join his people. My girls wondered if I knew him already from around the hood. I didn't, but I did like what I had just seen tonight. I hope that poor woman wasn't his woman because if she is, she's going to be upset when she call and I'm lying next to him.

"Damn, Shane. Girl who the hell is that man looking all fine and shit?"

I glanced back over to their table that sat at the opposite corner from our table.

"Robin girl, I don't know. He must like what he see so he decided to come my way I guess; and can you blame him, look at all this slim and trim and he sitting over there with a fat ass woman."

We all started laughing and clowning the woman that was still hanging all over him.

"Why she gotta be fat just because she ain't as small as your ass?"

I knew Keke was about to go on one. She thinks every time I'm talking about a fat woman I'm talking about her ass.

"Keke don't start no shit. You know damn well I wasn't talking about your ass or anyone else at this table for that matter."

Keke looked like she was about to speak until the waitress came over and took our orders. We all ordered the steak platter, which comes with T-bone steak, diced potatoes, eggs any way you like them and your choice of waffle or French toast. We all grabbed the French toast with ours and the house lemonade.

"Whatever Shane. All I know is, whenever we out you start clowning women who aren't a size ten and that shit ain't cool, especially in my presence."

Keke was about to chew nails and we go back a long time, at least ten years. I never want to upset her and I knew just what would make her happy.

"You wanna take a walk with me to the bathroom Keke?"

I knew she would. I just asked to be polite. She didn't even say nothing. She just got up from the table and walked back pass the cashier to the bathroom. We stepped in and made sure the coast was clear. Once that was done, I reached in my gold and black Michael Kors purse and pulled out her little bag of heaven.

Keke's eyes lit up like a Christmas tree. She held out her hand and watched me drop her sanity into it. She walked up a little closer to me just enough to kiss me on the lips. We have kissed many times so this was no different except this time she was a little in her feelings.

"Thanks Shane. You know just what to do to get me right and this will truly get me right."

This time she went in for a full blown tongue kiss and sucking of the lips. I may talk about fat women from time to time but this is one fat ass that I've never had a problem with.

"Just ease up with the shit Shane, I don't like hearing you speak like that especially when I'm a big woman myself. Regardless if I'm not as big as the other women you make fun of I'm still considered a big girl."

I smiled knowing she had to get that same speech off of her chest.

"And you wear it well my dear."

She made a pouty face letting me know that she wasn't buying my shit this time.

"Okay Keke, you're right. I'll behave and sorry if I made you feel any type of way by running my mouth."

We walked back to our table but not before Keke sampled a little bit of heaven. I never judge my friends because one thing for sure and two for certain, everybody has demons. I would rather them get their shit from me than somebody in the streets who could be trying to get one over on them and plus people don't want everyone knowing their business. All my friends that cop from me know that I will and have kept their secrets. Even my girl Storry has dipped her finger in a little white heaven. I'm not trying to fuck off my money either, I could care less about who getting high. This is not my only hustle, it's just a little hustle until I finally find the nerve to open my own restaurant.

"Damn y'all asses been gone for a minute. Got me sitting here like a raga muffin."

We all laughed at Robin. She was the funny one of the group, always cracking jokes so carefree and like myself and Keke she has no kids either. She was tall and slim and kissed by the midnight sky. She wore a long weave, parted down the middle and she had high cheek bones. She didn't have a big but or big breast, everything on her body was just a handful and she was happy with that.

Keke's ass just need to calm down. She's a beautiful woman. Yes she's thicker than most but I never cared, she has always said that her size eighteen was a perfect size. She was short, caramel brown complexion with the cutest dimples in each cheek. She wore her size well. I've seen men and women throw themselves at her on many occasions. I've seen her accept some of them and dismiss some of them, so I never knew why she always seemed to be tripping when I start running my mouth.

Yes I was proud of my little size ten frame. I thought I was the perfect size that no man or woman for that matter would say no too. I don't care what size they claim to be more attracted to. When it comes to my tight plump ass, firm round breast and small waist, I get the attention of many. When a man says, oh, I just love me some big girls, before that sentence come out of their mouth my lean legs be wrapped around their waist.

My complexion was golden bronze. I didn't wear the weaves not that it matters. I always wore my natural styles whether it's in Bantu knots, fro, or flat ironed, I love my style. We all rocked our styles differently but we aren't in competition with each other.

Once our food came we chowed down like it was our last meal. I didn't pay Jerald any attention the whole time he was with his friends. The last time I glanced at Jerald, he was pushing that woman off of him. Her ghetto neck roll and finger waving let me know that she wasn't happy about it. My girls and I finished our food left a tip and bounced. I was tired, drunk and sleepy; we all were, so home was our next stop.

I reached my door. I was living in the hood which was all good with me. There's nothing like living in the hood. It was late; but because it was summer no one was in the house. It seemed like everyone was either just pulling up from the club or sitting out on their porches. The block wasn't loud, it was calm. You heard a little chatter coming from either direction but at three in the morning it was almost that time the block would be going to sleep.

Just like any other summer all the grown folks go to sleep just when the kids of the block start waking up. That shit gets on my nerves trying to sleep and you hear someone's bad ass kids outside at seven in the morning.

"What up Shane?"

I looked to my left as I walked towards my building.

"What up Terri?"

I continued to walk up the five steps to my building before I head Terri speed walking in my direction.

"Shane, baby you got something I can have?"

I was not interested in what Terri ass was on at this moment. I was tired and all I wanted to do was go to sleep. Her ass always want me to get her high for free then fuck her. That shit got boring real fast.

"I'm dry right now Terri. I won't have nothing until later on. That's when I'll come look for you."

I put the key in the door and pushed the door open. Right as I was closing it I heard Terri call my damn name again.

I paused trying to get my thoughts together to see if I was going to answer her or leave her ass standing in front of my gate. I turned and looked at this woman who was beautiful, short and slim. Her body was beautiful, but I couldn't fuck with someone who didn't take care of their fucking kids. I understand she would rather get high, but damn it if you don't want your kids give them to someone that could take better care of them than you could.

There was a time I walked in her house and saw that her son, who was only two sitting in the middle of the floor with a nasty ass diaper on, cereal stuck to his naked body and snot running down his nose. He was a mess and her house was a mess. The only reason she keeps herself up because like most women, she gotta use what she got to get what she want.

"You want some company Shane?"

I knew that Terri ass was going to ask me some shit like this and now I have to be the bad guy.

"I'm good Terri. You go in the house and keep an eye on your son. I'll catch up to you tomorrow."

I didn't even give her chance to say anything else. I walked my ass in and closed the door. I didn't want to have shit to do with Terri ass. I guess I should've thought about that shit before I let my mouth take her pussy on a ride of a lifetime.

Cornelius

It was already the middle of the week and the damn weekend passed me by yet again. I tell you, having your own business is challenging. Especially when it takes a front seat to your social life, which I don't have. I tried to get shorty from the Walmart to come by this morning. She said she would but I think she has stood me up just to get back at me for not responding to her text. It's cool, I don't have time for games today or tomorrow. However, I do need some wet, wet.

Walking into my office which wasn't very big, it had just what I needed to look professional and conduct business on so many different levels. Soon as you walk in there is a counter to greet people, about two feet further were two offices that sat across from each other. I used one as my personal office and the other was a board room where I held meetings. It could hold at least fifteen people comfortably. There was an oval shaped wooden-glossed over table with chairs around the walls. The walls had a few pictures of properties I've bought, restored and sold, placed strategically on them.

My office was black and cranberry. I hadn't thought nothing of the color scheme until this woman I was messing around with showed me how well the two went together.

My desk was black with a cranberry stained glass on top. Two high back leather chairs sat in front of it and of course I had the master high back boss chair. The bathroom was further back as well as the junk closet, as I call it.

I was ready to get the morning started when I heard someone knock on the front door. I waited to see if they would leave but the knock got stronger. I walked out of my office and saw a female standing there. I didn't make her out until I got a lot closer. Once I opened the door I was already smiling. My girl Shane was standing there smiling just as hard.

"Where the hell your key?" I asked. I opened the door and watched her walk in.

"Man I was fucking rushing this morning while I was trying to gather everything. I had my house key thinking it was my work key. Shit, I'm just glad that you're here so I don't have to call and stand outside; like I'm trying to get picked up and pay next months' rent."

We both laughed. Shane's just a real good friend. She was one of the girls from the block that was actually trying to get her shit together. She wasn't trying to fuck me and I wasn't trying to fuck her. She told me that she goes both ways. While it was intriguing, I just wasn't interested like that. She wasn't looking for a man to put her on. She had some stumbles like everyone has, but she didn't let that stop her. So when I decided to get this business I knew exactly who I wanted to be my right hand man or in this case, woman.

Shane has an athletic type of body. Even though she was medium built, I swear the girl didn't look like she had an ounce of fat on her body. Her complexion was beautiful minus a few dark spots she has from severe acne. She say she play ball a lot and run every morning. I can remember when she said she started running, it was to out run the demons that were trying to attack her. She didn't want to kill, rob, or hurt anybody; but according to her, the voices kept calling her.

At one point she had no job and no money other than her side hustle. We both knew you could only do that shit for so long, she had rent like everybody else. She said she had a friend that put her on. From what she tells me, the friend does this full-time low key. Shane said she just needed a pick me up, a few months later I started this company and brought her on. I wasn't aware of her problems at the time but I quickly found out. I'm here to help my people any way I possibly can.

After getting in and settled Shane made sure I had my coffee, notes and my breakfast. She always made this Cajun shrimp and grits with a touch of Gouda cheese; this woman had skills. She brought them in these glass bowls. I've always thought she was in the wrong business; she should have been a caterer.

"Girl you know you in the wrong business, this shit be too damn good."

I walked into my office smiling from ear to ear, with my food.

As the day was starting for us here, I see I had a meeting in an hour. I didn't recognize the person that was on the email.

"Shane, who is Ms. Rogers?"

Shane went to look at her email that she sent me.

"Oh, that's a woman who's looking to sell her home. She says it's run down and she don't have funds to fix it. She say it's time for her to get out of Chicago anyway so she contacted you."

While Shane continued to busy herself with the daily running of the company, I stayed in my office going over paper work that would allow me to buy more properties to sell or rent dirt cheap. I've never been about ripping off my people. I know we all have it hard. No matter how many coins you may have in the bank, when fighting in this world of devils, it takes a lot more than money. It's going to take unity of our people. I'll do my part by making them feel like they can live a life that they want without being ripped off.

"Cornelius, Ms. Rogers has just walked in."

I looked at my watch and told her to give me a couple of minutes. Shortly after, Ms. Rodgers was walking into my office. I almost hit the fucking floor when I looked up from my desk. I held my composure and wondered what game this was.

Tessa walked in and was smiling from ear to ear. She made me smile just by looking at her light up the room. I know she's gotten a bad rap from certain people that know her intimately but I don't give a damn, outside of sex she's a true friend. Hell, I would've let her come here and work but she said she had other things going on.

"Hey Cee or should I say Cornelius?"

Tessa walked over to me with arms opened wide and I accepted her hug.

"As always you can call me whatever you like. Come, step into the conference room."

As we walked over to the conference room I asked Shane to hold all my calls. I lead the way as she followed. Once the door was closed behind us, I was wondering why she wanted to come to the office to see me like this, instead of calling like she has done most of the time.

She took a seat in the first chair next to the head chair. I peeped what she had on which for her was nearly next to nothing. I tell you one thing, as a big girl she don't give a shit. She definitely wears what the fuck she wants to. She wore a knee length, black satin pencil skirt with bare legs and an off the shoulder satin ruffle shirt that flared at the bottom. And like all women, she had her come fuck me pumps on.

"Let me get straight to the point of why I'm here. First, I came like this because I haven't been able to reach you in a week and that was unusual. Second I have to let you know, the chick you met at Walmart a few days ago is my best friend."

I was stunned. I didn't know what to say at that very moment. It's not like Tessa and I are a couple but I don't want her to think that I'm some type of dog ass nigga, especially since I have put all that shit behind me.

"Storry is your home girl?"

Tessa nodded her head yes. "I'm not here to cause any problems. You know that's not my get down. But I do want you to know before that time comes and you take her down. How's that going to affect us?"

I couldn't believe what I was hearing. I know Chicago is small but damn, it ain't that damn small.

"At this point, Tessa, I've only met your home girl a few days ago and then I only talked to her once on the phone. I did ask her to come over this morning if she wasn't busy. That was about three hours ago. So I don't know what's up with her nor do I care to put more attention in it than it needs to be."

I saw the look on Tessa's face trying to inhale every word that I was saying as though she was getting full off of my truth. We've never lied to each other and I refuse to start that shit now.

"Okay Cee, I hear what you saying. I thought I just run this pass you."

"Did you tell your home girl that you know me?"

"Nope. I was waiting to see how far she was going to let this go on?"

Her answer confused me.

"I'm confused by your answer. What do you mean let this go on?"

Tessa adjusted herself in her seat a few times starting to look agitated. Before she could speak I ask did she want something to drink. Of course she said yes. Tequila and orange juice was her choice of drink. After I made her drink at the bar in the conference room, she took a few sips, then seemed to be relaxed immediately afterwards.

"My girl Storry's not that sit around and wait for one man, or woman for that matter, kind of woman. She has expressed how handsome you are and what not but she does have her pickings to choose from."

I nodded my head without a care in the world. It's not like I don't have pickings to choose from either. I don't even know the girl like that. But what I do require is that anyone that I talk to be up front and honest.

Tessa and I finished talking and drinking. She told me that she was trying to get her life right and since her twins were born she'd been waiting on a man that would never come back to her. I guess that 'get under a new man to get over an old man' shit don't really work. I gave Tessa the best advice that I could give her. I told her maybe she should go get in a program to help get that monkey off her back. She thought she was strong enough to handle that on her on.

I was now curious to know if Storry's ass was the honest type. Granted we saw each other in a parking lot and there was no time to really disclose anything. I'm going to give her the benefit of the doubt. I'm going to tell her a few things about the women I've had and see if she adds to it. I don't need to know her whole life history. I just don't want to be blindsided when and if and ex pops up later on and start tripping on her or me. Then I'm going to have to show whomever it is what that west side of Chicago life is all about.

Tessa and I ended our conversation with her giving me some bomb ass head. I wanted to dig up in her guts but I had another meeting soon. She didn't care, she knew I'd be around shortly to take care of her needs like no other.

Storry

I can't believe that I stood Cornelius up. Granted, I don't owe him nothing, but I could've at least sent him a text saying that I'll take a rain check.

Demetrius called and nothing else mattered. Once he got here I was super happy. I don't see him much but when I do, I always make sure he and I get that moment in. That time that never seems to erase itself from my memory. No matter how many times I have brought it up, he stays consistent with not being anyone's man.

I guess when you know that you're not relationship material then it's easy to move about the world without knowing you're hurting women.

I just semi met him only a few days ago and I think going all out too damn soon is ridiculous. I know damn well he's not thinking of me like that. Far as I know, he got babies and hoes everywhere and I don't need to be anyone else's notch on their belt. I let Demetrius get away with that shit but he's the one and only that shit will fly with. I fuck with men and occasionally women but when it's time for me to settle down, I'm going strickly-dickly at that point.

I've been wanting Demetrius ass for as long as I can remember and I'm not going to lie, I thought giving him some pussy would make him automatically change and fall madly in love with me. Man I couldn't have been so wrong. He came over late one Wednesday night which through me because I had to work the next morning, but for him I would take off if need be. At the time he thought that we needed a sit down face to face conversation. I didn't know about what so I agreed and let him come over.

That man walked his fine ass into my home and I immediately got aroused. I had the music on, some soft melodies and of course I had my wine on chill. He didn't drink, his vice was weed. After our pleasantries I poured me a glass a wine and watched him spark up his blunt. We sat on the sofa and he began to speak.

"Storry, look you're a fucking fabulous woman. Any man would be lucky to have a go getter like yourself on their arm. As for me, I just can't and don't do the relationship thing. It has nothing to do with you, it's all me. I've never wanted a relationship and as great as you are, I don't want one now."

I was dumb founded. I didn't know what to say. I didn't think he was going to drop a bomb like this on me. I really thought he was going to tell me that he would be going back out of town so I wasn't prepared for this kind of heart break.

"Wow, I don't know what to say except, okay."

I took another sip which turned into a gulp of my wine.

"Storry, please talk to me. We've been dealing with each other for a while now and I want your input on the matter at hand. Please baby, say something other than okay."

At that point, I wanted to throw my drink in his face, yell and scream down on him, but the boss chick rose up in me and I took another approach.

"Look, Demetrius, we've been having a ball and the great sex is just one hell of a bonus. However, I'm not looking for a relationship either. Now don't get me wrong, I do want one at some point but just not right now. Your touch has been mesmerizing, your conversation has been intellectual and stimulating, your sex, mind blowing is an understatement to say the least but the words haven't even been invented yet.

We'll see each other when we can, make the best out of it and go on with our lives."

He had a smirk on his face then he inhaled the smoke from his blunt and let it dance in his mouth before exhaling. He watched my eyes intently. I had nothing for him to see other than the words I have just spoken.

"Well it seems like we're on the same page which is a good thing because I don't want to hurt you Storry. I'm very much into you and I don't want to lose you as a friend no matter what. I just hope the next time I'm in town that I can come over and see you."

Right then and there I wanted to tell him to go to hell and no you can never come and see me. However, I went against that.

"You can come over whenever you blow into town. Just give me a heads up so I can be ready. In more ways than one."

We both laughed.

I continued to sip on my wine knowing that I just played the right hand to keep him coming back for more. The love that I started feeling for him in such a short time was unbelievable. I went with my feelings until he shot them down. I knew this was going to erk my damn nerves not knowing who he was fucking and no matter what he says, this whole no relationship is so he can have sex with as many women he wants.

It's cool though. I knew damn well I was playing the game with him and I wasn't going to get benched just because of feelings. Fuck that, watching him come and go was like watching Idris Elba walk in and out of a room. At thirty-two, he got his shit together and he in the real-estate business as well. Shit, maybe I need to get into that shit, I could use a change. Don't get me wrong, I make good money driving buses but real estate may be where I need to be.

Shane

I knew I should've called Jerald. I know he said he was with his kids and I want no parts of that. I mean I don't hate kids, I just don't want to be momma to nobody; not even a man's kids that I'm dealing with. I've heard some shit about his baby momma. On one hand I hear that she's cool people then on the other hand I hear that she look like a gorilla in a dress. I know damn well I'm far from anything like that so I don't see what the fuck Jerald see in her. On top of that, fucked her raw and made a baby with her.

I spoke with him briefly about it and he said it was a drunken night and they hooked up. I understand the whole I hooked up shit but in order for her to get pregnant he must have slept with her more than once. All that it was a drunken night, he can miss me with all of that. It's not like

I really care, I just don't like when people try and play me like I'm stupid.

I looked over on my dresser and it was almost time for me to get ready for work. I meant to ask Cornelius who the woman was that he had a meeting with. Especially since he seemed like he didn't even know his dam self.

I have to remember to ask him later on when he comes into the office today. I jumped out of bed to prepare for my day. After my shower I oiled up, through on some black skinny jeans, black tank top and a purple short waist fitted blazer. Through on some black and purple accessories. Grabbed my coconut oil and pulled my hair into an afro puff, pulled to the back. Other than some eyeliner and lip gloss that was all I needed. I had one hour to get to work, not that he cared if I was late.

I had some chicken strips marinating so I fried some of them and covered them with a sweet and spicy sauce, and paired them with light and fluffy waffles. I knew that he would love it. He never eats from the restaurant. He always wants me to cook which I'm cool with. Sometimes if I'm running late and didn't have time to cook he would let me leave just so I can go home and cook. Shit that was mad love if you ask me.

I packaged up all of my food and headed to my car. As soon as I got in and started it up, my phone started going off. I looked before pulling off and saw that it was my girl Storry.

"Hey boo. What's good?"

"Hey my sexy boo. I just need to know can I get some heaven, I'm running low."

"Girl please, you know I got you. You know at some point I gotta stop this petty ass shit and start doing something worthwhile."

I was tired of finding a local connects, making a deal with him, and then going back selling a little bit to this person and that person.

"I hear you sweetie, I was just thinking that I needed to go into the Real Estate business. Seems like that's where the money's at."

"When you're ready let me know. I can introduce you to my boss. He runs a Real Estate business and doing quite well for himself."

"Damn girl. What's all that noise I hear in the back ground?"

"I'm on my way to work and some damn fool pulled out just as this other car was speeding down a fucking one way street."

"Okay boo, I'm not going to hold you. I just wanted to let you know what I need."

"No problem boo. I can get that to you later on when I get off."

We hung up the phone and I drove the fifteen minutes to work. Half way to the job I got another call. I thought it was damn early for my phone to start going off like this. I looked at it and saw that it was, Do Not Answer. Whenever I see that number I don't answer, no matter what. I don't give a fuck, this mother fucker right here literally holds your heart in his hand and feeds it back to you. No thank you!

I dismissed that call and arrived to work. I opened the office because Cornelius wasn't in yet. Granted it was only 9 in the morning, I wasn't expecting him until a couple hours later. I placed his food in the oven in the back. Thank goodness we had a full kitchen back there. I settled in and started with the emails.

Going through the emails I saw an email from Ms. Rogers again. It was only a couple of days since she was here last so I guessed Cornelius bought her property. I clicked on the email being nosey and I was shocked at the contents.

I really had a great time with your dick in my mouth the other day. We must see each other more often if you not going to be seeing my girl Storry. I would love to give you what you been missing.

I couldn't believe my damn eyes. Don't get me wrong, I don't care who Cornelius fuck around with but this chick named my girl and now I'm curious. Looks like I'll let Storry know ASAP!

Hell I didn't even know she even knew Cornelius. I could call her later but my nosey ass want to know right damn now. I grabbed my phone after sending all the emails to Cornelius. Finally after the third ring Storry finally answered.

"Hey girl what's up?"

"Girl I know I just talked to you, but I'm at work and need to ask you a question."

"What's that?"

"To my surprise I didn't know you and Cornelius were an item. He's my boss but you're my girl, and I just found out that he's sleeping with someone else."

Storry was quiet for a few seconds before speaking.

"Well this is some shit. I didn't even know you knew Cornelius and just for the record, I don't know him like that. I just met him less than a week ago, so he's free to live his life as I live mines. But just out of curiosity, who's the female?"

"Yeah, the realty company I work for is his, and as far as the female goes I only have her last name which is Rogers."

"Rogers? That damn name don't even ring a bell with me. What did she look like?"

"Girl she had on a black skirt and some heels. She had on a red shirt, I really didn't see her face all that well because she had on one of those, going to church on Easter Sunday hats on and some big sunglasses, and she dark-skinned.

"Oh well, like I said. We met less than a week ago so who he's doing is his business."

"I hear that. So like we talked about earlier, I'll hit you up when I get off for what I asked for."

We talked a little bit more before we hung up. Hell I knew my boss was good looking but it looks like he's going to have a problem on his hands.

The day went fast as usual. I love working for Cornelius, he don't trip. I can practically come and go when I want except when he's having a meeting.

What I do need to do before I get up with Storry is catch up with Jerald ass.

Jerald has been MIA since he had the kids. It's only Tuesday and I know damn well he's taken them kids home already. It's not like she doing something so important that she can't have her own kids.

I don't know what kind of game Jerald's trying to play but I damn sure don't want no parts of it. If I did, then I would answer Mr. Do Not Answer. And that shit's not going to happen!

Jerald

I still can't believe I have the kids, not that I care. I love my damn kids! I'm just more surprise that Tessa ass hasn't even blown my damn phone up with phony antics to get me to come over, with or without the kids. I wanted to call her but Shane called me first. I haven't heard from her since I went and got the kids, so I knew this wasn't going to be a pleasant phone call. I watched her name and face appear on the screen. I studied it for a minute before answering.

"Damn! Didn't seem like you were going to answer your phone."

Right then I just wanted to hang up on her ass.

"Well as you can see I did answer. So what's up other than your attitude?"

"Jerald don't fucking play with me. I haven't heard from your ass in a couple of days and you acting all nonchalant about it. So I need to know why?"

"No other reason other than I have my kids and when I'm with them I'm with them. They're still small so they need all of my attention."

"Jerald please! Your kids are seven that's not that small. And they do have to go to sleep whether it's nap time or night time, that's when you could've call."

"Shane, this conversation is redundant. How and what I do when I'm with my kids is my business. I told you getting a bigger place for us is what I'm striving for. I've also been looking for jobs, so excuse me if I've been too damn busy getting my shit right to entertain your ass."

I tell you whenever a man starts changing for the better it's always some broad that can't handle it. Especially if it is not all about her. I could care fucking less, I want a better life for me and my kids and selling

drugs ain't it.

"A job! Negro please! Other than selling drugs like

the rest of us, what can you possibly do? I mean not to rain

on your parade but you have to have this little thing called

experience now a days to even be considered for a gig.

What experience do you have?"

I wasn't about to be worried about this pussy

licking ass bitch. See the devil always send a muthafucka in

to take you off course; but not this time.

"Shane, don't let that little shit you serve to a few

lick'em friends make you think you actually out her selling

drugs. You're not out here taking penitentiary ass chances

like us real dope dealers. As I sit here and listen to this shit

you're spewing, I realize that me being on a totally

different page isn't sitting well with you, so lets' just fuck

when we see each other and let it be that. Because what I

won't do is sit here and listen to, too much more of how my hood nigga ass won't ever amount to shit other than what I am right now." I didn't even give her ass a second to respond. I clicked the end button.

Like most men that love pussy, they love fucking whenever possible and when Shane's ass was ready to give it up, I took her up on that. Somehow she has equated that to us dating and I never signed up for that. We cool and all but after I went to get my kids I'm just on a different page now.

If kids don't help you get your shit together then something is really wrong. Me living in a small ass apartment is just not what I want for me and mines. I can't be like Tessa's ass, don't have no job so the government gives her assistance. Now she gets a nice a place to call home, money for her bills; if she has any, and food stamps to buy as many steaks as she likes. My black ass has no job, all the government do for me is tell me to go find one or risk being locked up for non-payment for the kids I fucked for.

Since this drug shit is drying up I decided to go look for some factory jobs. At least they don't run no back ground check. I actually got hired at Pepsi Cola in the warehouse. I didn't even tell Shane that shit because it was clear she wouldn't give a fuck anyway. The company called me yesterday. The only people I told was my mom, kids, and my home boy Demetrius.

I only told Demetrius because he's been trying to get me out of the game to go into Real Estate with him. I didn't want no handouts then and I don't want one now. He told me he was in town so we agreed to meet up, smoke a few blunts and talk about these sorry ass women out here.

Living on the west side of the Chi was something I had grown tired of so it was only right that I made a change to get myself to a better level in my life. I know damn well

Tessa's not going to want to hear me say nothing about keeping my babies but dammit I'm not going to be a part-time daddy. Hell, I know she have men traffic in her house but my kids need to see their daddy's face on a regular, not random.

It's summer time and I want the kids to stay with me for the rest of the summer. Maybe tha'll help Tessa get her shit together, so our kids can have two parents that they're proud of. She act like all that damn drinking isn't a problem and I'm here to tell her at damn near thirty, she needs to do better. I've always been a dope boy making enough money for the latest clothes, shoes, and bullshit.

I'm tired of taking penitentiary chances and for what, to look like I have more than I have. Shit, that has grown cold just like the dope game. I see muthafuckas out here slanging that shit and still living with their momma or driving their woman's car. That shit don't add up so changing my shit up was the only thing I knew to do.

Hell, I may be even crazier to tell Tessa if she get her shit together, I just may be inclined to give her what she wants. And that's for us to be a family. I mean hell, everyone already know that I smashed and yes she does have a fucked up reputation but we could move somewhere no one knows either of us and start over. Easier said than done. All I know at this moment is, I'm ready to start putting shit in order and I really don't care who with me or not. I did need to talk to Tessa and ask her a question. I really didn't want to have this conversation but it needed to be done.

I grabbed my phone off the end table while the twins were taking a nap. This was a great time to holla at my baby momma. She must've been sitting by the phone because she answered on the first ring.

"Hey Jerald. What's going on? How are my babies?"

"The babies are fine. Check this out, I wanted to run something by you."

"I'm listening."

"I wanted to know can I keep the twins for the rest of the summer? You've had them since they were born and I just want to do my part."

There was a ten second pause at least before she spoke.

"Of course you can Jerald. They're your kids just as much as they're mine. I've never tried to keep them from you. I just wanted you to have a job or something steady while having them."

Ain't this bitch got some nerve! She don't have a fucking job and if it weren't for section 8, she wouldn't have shit steady either. I tell you muthafuckas live off the government and swear their doing it themselves.

"I didn't call you to hear your judgments, I'm not judging you. It must make you feel as if your shit together to judge me, huh?"

I swear I didn't have time for this shit.

"That's not what I'm saying or at least that's not what I'm trying to say. I know my shit fucked up. You don't have to remind me. I just know that I want the best for our kids; that's it, that's all."

"Well its mid-June so I just wanted to check with you and I'm glad you said yes. Thanks Tessa."

"Oh Before you go, do you need to come get them some clothes and stuff?"

I told her that I would buy them some clothes. That gives me another chance to take them shopping and see for myself what they like and what they don't. She sounded a little upset. I knew that was just another one of her ways to get me to come over so she can try anything to get me to sleep with her. The crazy shit is, she and I both know that if I wanted to get up with her in that way, I could've had her at any time I wanted.

Demetrius

Now I know Shane's ass seen my phone call. Every time I come into town I hit her up and all my calls go unreturned. I don't know what the hell is up with that. The only thing that I can say is like so many others, she got hung up on me and knew I wasn't into making no woman mines.

Either they were going to hang with the way shit is or they wasn't. I haven't heard about her being with anyone so other than that, I would like to speak to her and see what the fuck is her problem. And I really don't give a fuck all like that to begin with.

I talked with my boy Jerald, he told me he was happy that he finally got him a legit job. I was happy for him too, because all the nickel and diming shit was played the fuck out.

I still kept my place here in Chicago. Only because I wasn't about to go to no hotel in my own home town. As soon as one of these women know you in town without your own place, they quick to start in on the, *you can come stay with me shit.* I don't know what the fuck that shit's all about, especially when they all know the same damn thing.

I know I just saw Storry yesterday, but I do have to make my rounds. I called up a very sweet woman who taste even better. Sitting on the edge of my sofa, I found her number in my contacts and press the call button. It took a matter of seconds to for her to answer her phone.

"Hey baby, I heard you were in town. How are things going?"

"Things are going just fine, I'm going to be in town for another day or two and I just wanted to slide in on you if possible?"

"It's always possible my love. You still have the address right?"

"Yeah."

"When were you thinking about coming over?"

"In about an hour."

"See you then, my love."

I hung up the phone knowing that was a guaranteed fuck. I try my best to tell everyone that I come in contact with that I don't want a woman but most women, they think all they have to do is give me the pussy and I'll change my fucking mind. If I did want a woman, I would and could've had one by now. I just can't deal with the attitudes, the mood swings and now a days with these bitches in the streets no more. That's drama I don't have time for.

Being into Real Estate allows me to travel everywhere. Most of the time I work with my home boy

Cornelius; who I have to talk to because I could've sworn I saw him about a week ago in a parking lot talking to Storry.

I look for shit in other cities and states or Cornelius sends me leads to these places. He gets them and flips them and I get my sixty percent cut, I'm good with that. I could have started my business long ago, but I started loving to travel way too much to be sitting up in a damn office pushing papers.

I hopped in the shower, through on some True Religion black jeans and black matching tee-shirt, and white gold watch. I made sure I put the smell good on so I grabbed that new joint Eros by Versace, brushed my waves, grabbed my keys and headed out the door.

My truck is a black on black Cadillac Escalade. The sun was still beaming and the block was busy. I couldn't get to my truck for speaking to everyone and the one person I didn't want to speak to was heading my way.

I was speaking with one of the home boys from the block and I cut our conversation short just so I can hop in my truck and by pass Yollanda's ass. I didn't even get my music going, I just sped off. I saw her turn on her heels when she saw that I had just ignored her ass. I was ready to get on the road and get to my destination.

The streets were filled with all sorts of people. Kids walked with bags of candy in their hand. Music roared out of most of the cars that either passed or was sitting at a light. There was nothing like summer time in Chicago. I don't care who you ask they will agree.

Fifteen minutes later the clock in the truck read five and I was at my destination. Once I walked up to the door, I rang the doorbell. It didn't take but mere seconds for the door to fly open and there she stood.

Looking like a whole fucking snack. She was smiling from ear to ear. I was smiling my damn self but I didn't let it show too much. She stepped to the side and I walked in like I was paying the rent. Once the door was closed behind me, I turned to her and kissed every part of her skin that was visible.

"Damn Tessa, I damn near was speeding to get over here. I feel like it's been way to long."

"Yes indeed, it has been too damn long. The last time you were here I think it was six months or so and the kids and I were at your house for the weekend. You made us feel right at home, but what I want to know is why the hell have you been away so long and don't give me that it's work crap either."

I couldn't keep shit from Tessa, even if I wanted to. Other than really good friends and regardless of her habits, I could really confide in her when need be.

I took a seat at the counter and sat in the bar stool. Tessa came to sit next to me and asked what was up. I didn't want to have to disclose my personal business like this especially since I came here to get some and not air out my dirty laundry.

"Tessa, look I've been going through a lot over the last year and I've just really been keeping myself busy so I don't have to think about my personal shit."

Tessa gave me this confused look because she knew I was beating around the bush.

"Spit it out Demetrius. You know there's a no judgement law in my life. I'm the mother of one of your closest friends and you and I are occasionally sleeping together, so I'm never here to judge."

I took a deep breath and aired my dirty laundry.

"I'm HIV positive. I felt something was wrong a little over a year ago. I started having night sweats, nausea, diarrhea and all sorts of other things and I dealt with that shit for about six months before going to the doctor. Figuring that I was coming down with a cold or something."

Tessa just looked at me with sorrow and pity in her eyes. Just like me, she like to fuck whoever, whenever and I was terrified that I could've passed this shit on to her.

"I'm really sorry that you're going through this. I guess that was part of the problem when you left here last time, you had a fever and what not."

"Yeah, I'm just scared that I may have passed this shit to you."

"How?"

"What do you mean how? We've been sleeping together for a year now."

"And unless you got amnesia, we've never slept together without a condom either. As much as I wanted to you never did so I didn't push, sleeping with you protected has been the best decision I've ever made, especially considering your situation now."

"Damn, I completely forgot that out of all the women I sleep with I've never smashed you unprotected. Damn, I'm happy for that especially with the kids. I know I can be a dog ass dude but I never would have wanted to give this shit to you."

Tessa smiled as I was about to fix me a drink.

"I must ask. Have you seen and slept with Storry ass?"

"In fact I have. But I did sleep with her protected. I didn't even let her give me head."

Tessa and I continued to talk about my bullshit and her bullshit. I had to tell her that I didn't want Storry to come to my house because of the spare room I use for her and the kids. I didn't feel like lying again. Even though we all have demons of some sort, I just had to start letting mine out; keeping this shit in was about to kill me.

Tessa showed her concern for me and to be honest I was cool. I had my meds so I'll be okay. If Magic Johnson could be cured, so can I. I was really thinking about being able to live a normal life and continue doing what I do. Some people would think that having this shit would slow them down. Well not me, I wasn't trying to be no one's pity case.

We slapped bellies before I left and since I don't like head with condoms on I didn't let Tessa do that. We agreed that all was good between us and Tessa assured me that me having HIV wouldn't change anything. That was obvious since we just smashed. I see why most people don't fuck with her outside of sex and it's only because of her weight, dark skin and that scar, but when you look past that she's a down ass chick.

Storry

Cornelius and I finally talked about meeting up. It only took a week after meeting him in Walmart that I thought that it was time that I gave him my goodies. Even though I've already gotten my tires rotated by Demetrius, I still wanted to see what Cornelius had to work with.

Once I got to his home he had drinks on ice, music playing in the back ground and his home smelled delicious. I can't believe he cooked as well. I let my purple fitted mini summer dress hug my body and show off my shapely legs. My hair was in a messy bun while my ears and neckline adorned purple and silver accessories.

We sat down in the kitchen and I was offered practically any drink that I could think of. I settled for a pineapple margarita. I was surprised to see that he knew how to make it. I told him to add another shot of tequila to mines, I needed more tabasco with my hot sauce.

Our conversation was great. We talk about the community and ways to improve and what he's doing to be a vast part of that change. We discussed this bullshit ass President, relationships and this was a first. Most men don't or can't even have intellectual conversations, this was really refreshing. I don't know what he got up his sleeve but I was already hooked. The music played beautiful melodies of Jill Scott, India Arie and those alike.

"It smells so good in here what do you have cooking?"

"Well I don't have anything cooking; I stopped off and got a little soul food for us from my restaurant. Baked and fried chicken, greens, sweet potatoes, mac and cheese, you know the works. I didn't know what you like but I figured I couldn't go wrong with these menu choices."

"You're exactly right. You can't go wrong with these choices. I'm starved and ready to eat. On top of that, this damn pineapple margarita is starting to work on me. I'm starting to feel tingly."

Cornelius smiled and took a sip of whatever clear liquor he had in his drinking glass. He pulled the food out of the oven that he had already put in dishes and platers. I was impressed that he just didn't pull out the damn Styrofoam containers. He fixed my plate once his plate was made. We said a quick silent prayer then dug in.

This food was so damn good I was already thinking about seconds before I was even done with the first. I knew that with this good food and great drinks that he was in for some damn good dessert. As we continued to talk I found out a little more about his business and the people that he works with and to my surprise I didn't know he knows Demetrius.

"I must say that I'm surprised to know that you know Demetrius, I mean he's been a friend of mine for a while now."

I saw the look of uncertainty in his face but I wasn't about to put my foot in my mouth.

"Yeah me and Demetrius go back a ways. I mean when I got into this Real Estate thing I reached back and got the ones that I knew would want in on this lucrative business. So I must ask. Are you and Demetrius more than friends?"

I swallowed the last of my drink hard, not sure if I wanted to disclose my information to him like this.

"No, he's a great friend. Anytime I get to kick it with him when he comes to town is always a plus. I mean we go back about three years now." I tried to assure him that I have no secrets.

"Okay, I can deal with that. Just in case you're worried, I'm not going to ask him anything about y'all friendship."

I nodded my head and poured more liquor from the pitcher in my glass and we continued our meal.

Once the meal and drinks were consumed he gave me a tour of his home, very modest. Chocolate and brown furniture, black art on the walls, nothing fancy but very inviting. Cornelius made a gesture that we continue upstairs. I followed with my drink still in my hand. His bedroom was massive. Flat screen on the wall, bed seemed to go from one end of the wall to the next. This liquor was working on me and I knew that it was time for me to test the waters. After the tour, I was ready for the other tour, the kind that has me walking bow-legged afterwards.

We were back in his room and started a small conversation. He hit a button on his phone and music started playing. My hands started roaming, I didn't wait for him to touch me first, I caressed every inch of his body. He was built but not like he hit the weights every day. He was well toned and solid. Just like I like them.

As my hands roamed his body and my lips followed, I wasted no time getting to know his third leg. The length and width was a perfect fit for my mouth. I heard moans escape his mouth and I knew I was doing a great job, not that I worried that I wouldn't. He pulled me back up and my clothes started falling to the floor. My yellow flesh was his for the taking. He stood back for a few seconds and admired my beauty. Men seem to do that often. I saw the familiar smile creep across his full lips and I returned the smile. We rolled around his bed. Him on top, me on top, he wanted me to sit on his face, and we were making our own music and didn't give a fuck who heard us.

Sweat dripped from his forehead onto my face and neck as he slow stroked me. I must say that this was some good dick and I knew I was coming back for more. He told me how good I was over and over again. The more he said it, the more I put it on him when I was riding him or even if I rolled my hips when he was hitting me from the back. I knew I had to put my best foot forward and after he came twice, I knew my mission was complete.

We sat back and caught our breath with the starry eyed look we both gave each other. After laying there and loving the jumping jack feeling I was getting between my legs, I decided to get up and g get something to drink. Cornelius wanted me to bring him something and I told him to get it himself because I wasn't coming right back. Heading to the kitchen I admired the art that was on the staircase. I poured me a glass of juice and sat at the marble counter top scrolling Fakebook. Shortly Cornelius came down and saw that I was drinking my juice. I looked at him but that starry look he had previously, was gone. I didn't think nothing of it and kept right on doing what I was doing.

Minutes later my face was hitting the top of the counter. Thank goodness my hands were there to block a mightier blow. My hair was wrapped around his hand and I was tossed around like a fucking rag doll. All I could do was beg him to stop. The next thing I knew, I was getting tossed out the fucking house ass naked. I banged on the door for him to let me back in. Seconds after that my keys were getting thrown out of the window. I hurried to my car. I was so hurt and pissed that the hot leather seats didn't even bother me.

It took me longer than I would've liked it to getting home. Driving naked and bruised was embarrassing as fuck. I finally made it to my home after being stared at by folks either walking or driving by. I grabbed the sheet from my back seat that I have for people to sit on so my seats

don't get messed up. I wrapped the black sheet around me.
Being that it is summer time there were too many people
outside. I manned my shit up and walked my ass into my
apartment. Yeah they looked at me but I didn't bother to
look at them.

Once I was finally in the house, I dropped my sheet
to the floor and ran straight to the bathroom. I looked at
myself in the mirror and I was mortified at what I saw. This
dude whom I just met has bruised my fucking face by
slamming my head into the countertop. I had scratches on
my legs and arms from him throwing me outside into the
blazing ass sun. This has got to be some made for television
type of shit happening right now.

The only thing that kept running through my mind
was what did I fucking do? I couldn't come up with
anything that would have him treat me this way. I fucked
and sucked him just as he asked and had a great time at.

Then to my surprise the muthafucka was throwing me outside naked.

I feel so fucking stupid. Somewhere I missed that this man was a beast and I don't want any parts of him if this is how he treats women. I put my hand up to my head and felt the knot that was forming on the front of my damn forehead. I should take a fucking picture and show this asshole what he did.

I have dealt with some assholes in my day, but none of them has ever done anything like this shit to me. I was almost reluctant to call Demetrius so he could come handle this fool, but thought quickly against it, seeing I had just let him dig all up in my guts. I swear this has got to be one for the fucking books and wait until I call Tessa and tell her this shit. Hopefully, her hoe ass ain't fucking another random when I call.

Just when I start to think that I have it bad, I think of her ass and realize my shit could be a whole lot worse. I could've babies and shit with no good ass niggas and have the reputation of being the west side hoe. Anything in my life was better than hers.

I tried to let her know that Jerald wasn't the one she should be fucking with because he's no good. Did she listen? No. So I had to show her ass. Yeah, I let him fuck just to prove a point. I haven't gotten around to telling her. I actually didn't give a fuck to tell her anything after I saw no matter what, she was still going to be sleeping with him.

I have gotten off of track with my thoughts. Thinking about calling her got me thinking about shit I don't even give a fuck about. Let me focus on me and what I plan to do with his ass. As of right now, all I want to do is take a long hot bath and try and relax.

I ran my bath water. I got into it with some lavender Epsom salt to try and sooth my aches and pains. I think my fucking ego is bruised as well. I'm still in shock. I heard my phone ringing from the other room which also laid on the floor next to the sheet. I wanted to run and get it but also felt that I would regurgitate if I saw that it was him. First thing when I get myself together is to block that asshole.

Cornelius

I tell people to stop fucking with me in any kind of way, especially these smart mouth ass women. I've had a conversation with Storry about my temper and what I won't stand for. I guess just because she has a cute face and thick in the waist that she thinks she can ignore and or speak to me any way she feels.

I can only assume that getting thrown out on her community ass has woke her ass up when it comes to me. Now did I want to bang her head and throw her out naked? No. I did however, want to teach her a lesson and I hope she learned it. I just called a few minutes ago and after a few rings it went to voicemail.

I expected her not to answer my calls. I'll give her a day or two and hope that she comes to her senses and maybe we can start over. I've been trying to change my ways but it never seems to fail. After these women give you some pussy they start acting like they big time shit, and you're the same shit they wiped off the bottom of their shoe. I do feel kind of bad for throwing shorty out like that but she had it coming.

I watched her out of the upstairs bedroom window, she sat in her car for a few moments before driving off. I think I need to call up Tessa and give her a heads up to what just went down. I didn't want to involve her but after all Storry is her friend. Fuck it. I'm going to call and get this shit over with. I picked up my phone, scrolled through my call log and found Tessa's number. Her phone rang three times before I heard her voice on the other end.

"Hello."

"What up Tessa boo?"

"All good over here. Just walked a friend to the door. What's good with you? Haven't heard from since I left your office?"

"I know. I was meaning to get back at you but I've been busy. Enough about all that, I called to inform you that I had to throw your girl Storry out on her naked ass a little while ago." I poured me a drink while speaking.

"What you mean naked? Like y'all fucked then you through her out?"

"NO! It wasn't like that. Yes, we fucked but then I asked her to do something and she got smart mouthed with me like I'm that nigga that don't matter. So with that I had to make an example."

"Cornelius, I know your examples. What do you mean exactly?"

"I followed her to the kitchen where she was still acting like she got diamond pussy. I grabbed her by the back of her head with a hand full of hair and slammed it into the counter top. Then I dragged her off the bar stool and she made a naked exit out of my house. I did throw her phone and keys out the window though."

"Dammit Cornelius, you said you were not going to be putting your hands on these women anymore. You gone keep on and someone is either gone shoot your ass or call the police on you, just keep on. And I know Storry and I've been friends for a long time but now when she tells me the Storry I'm going to have to look all surprised. Damn you Cornelius."

"You know damn well I'm not worried about no fucking police and second, I wish a bitch would ever pull a gun on me. For her sake, she better know how to use it. What I care about sending a bitch to the morgue after she has pulled a gun on me, aint bout shit!"

Tessa and I kept on talking about everything and nothing until her other line rang. She informed me that it was in fact Storry, so she wanted to take the call. We hung up and I went back to my own thoughts. I sat down in the very same spot that Storry had sat almost two hours ago and just thought about me being too hard on her. I thought it over more than I cared to. Even Tessa has told me all the dirt that Storry's out her doing like nobody sees her sneaking around with my boy Demetrius, and whichever woman she chooses to be with at the moment.

It's not like any of that really bothers me, we've only known each other a short time. She's free to do her but I bet she'd feel differently if I told her I've been smashing Tessa for a while now and don't have no plans on stopping. That's unless Tessa decided she was ready to stop.

I have given Storry time after time to come clean about the extra shit she's doing, and since she won't break neither will I. I just want all women to understand that when I tell them some shit about me they better understand me good the first time.

If I wanted to be treated like a bitch with these women, I would. But I haven't found no pussy that damn spectacular that would have me gone that far. With my drink in my hand I began to walk back to my bedroom and change the sheets when my phone rang. I answered without even really looking at the number. I just knew that it was Storry.

"Storry!"

"Man, hell no this ain't no Storry! Who got your nose wide the fuck open?"

"Demetrius boy, what's up man?"

I haven't heard from my partner in crime in a while. Damn it was good to hear his voice.

"Man ain't shit to it. What's good with you man?"

"Chillling at the crib right now. Gon' be hitting the streets in a few. Shit, man we need to get up."

"Okay, that's cool. When you hit the streets of Chicago, hit my line. You know how I do. When I get back home it's some house calls I have to make."

"Boy you damn sho' aint changed a bit."

I laughed a hearty laugh after my statement. I know this man like the back of my hand when it comes to the ladies.

We agreed to meet up later then we hung up the phone. I continued to go to my room to change my sheets. I reached my bedroom and scanned my room. Just looking at the twist and turns of the sheets almost made be horny again.

I thought about the good sex I had just had with Storry. The room still had a faint smell of sex in the air that I inhaled deeply. I sat my drink on my night stand and began snatching the sheets and comforter off the bed. I threw them to the floor, went to my linen closet and retrieved a sexy red and grey set. I could care less about some fucking sheets but little shit like this turns women on.

A couple of hours later, I was on the streets of Chicago. The temperature was hot and I was ready to just chill. I was glad my boy was in town. We hit up the cigar bar to chill and catch up. We arrived at the same time, gave each other dap and a slight hug. We went in and since I'm a regular, we were walked up stairs to VIP were they serve you Louis XIII. This fine ass woman named Alexa was our server for tonight. Every time I see her I think about smashing, but because she on a come up from any man that she thinks has some money, she dives right in and ruin her own damn chances.

We were seated with a shot of Louis XIII in our glass and not to mention, a slither of Luey on our cigars that were now dry. Alexis cut our cigars for us, as we partook in some good conversation and smoke. I wish I had some weed in this damn cigar; that would've got me all the way together. But I'll have some real smoke when I leave out of here and hopefully catch up to Storry's ass so I can give her an apology. Me and Demetrius toasted and sipped.

"Damn man, it's truly good to see you. Looks like business is doing well for you?"

I was ready to tell my homeboy all about this chick Storry but thought against that. Just to make sure he hasn't smashed already. I know Storry gave me her version so I was going to play this shit out and see what he has to say, if anything.

"Same here man, and the truck just a little something I picked up a few months ago. Aint nothing to it."

After that statement Demetrius had himself another shot poured.

"The hell it ain't! Don't down play your accomplishments. Fuck! That's why we work as hard as we do so we can shine when we need or want to. Shit, I refuse to down play my shit."

"I hear you man. So what's been popping with you outside of work? I know there's some little cutie you got. So tell me the bullshit that may or may have not brought you out of retirement."

We both laughed at Demetrius question/statement.

"Damn man, you acting like you know me or something."

"I think ten years constitutes as knowing someone."

We both clanked our glasses together. I still didn't want to divulge Storry yet. I wanted to see who he's smashed since he been back first. I know it's petty but my homeboy Demetrius has a long list of women that he screw over and Chicago's not that damn big.

"Well you know I had to go see a couple so far and yes I smashed. I got one more on my list but her ass ain't answering my fucking phone calls. I don't know what I could've done to this woman to have her ignore my fucking calls."

"How about you have her do all kind of sex shit you like and then bounce on her. You know women are emotional. Once you part that greasy split, emotions just come pouring out."

"Man please, Shane know what time it is and I don't owe her shit. We gave each other the same damn thing…a nut. What the fuck she got to be tripping for?"

"Man, didn't I school you on the ways of women. You better start taking my fucking advice if you don't want these women taking a bat to your fucking car or worse, your head."

As we continued our drinking and got a few more refills, I see my boy never did say the woman he was sleeping with except for one that don't fucking matter. I would say if he didn't mention her then she may not be that damn important. After a few more drinks Demetrius started coughing and shit. He started sweating and I know damn well it wasn't hot in the cigar bar. So he excused himself and went to the bathroom.

I've never known him to choke on nothing but weed so I don't know what the fuck his problem is.

Alexis with her caramel skin was flawless, she did however have her ass plumped up and breast enlarged. I hope these women don't think their fooling no real men out here. She came over to ask would I need anything else since Demetrius had gone to the restroom. I nodded my head. I knew I would be seeing her later. Especially if Storry still hadn't come to her senses yet.

Shane

I don't know what the fuck Demetrius calling me for. The last time I saw him, I was on my knees begging him not to walk out of my front door and like so many other men; he walked. They all say the same damn shit about not wanting to be nobody's man. I don't recall him saying that when he was trying to fuck. I swore that I would never fuck with him again and especially after knowing he fuck with Tessa. Even though I've never seen the girl; not even a picture, just hearing stories about her makes me shake my damn head.

After he told me that he fuck with the type of women that will fuck and suck you no matter what, (Tessa) I could have threw the fuck up. It's not like it's hard to know who Tessa is. She has one of the biggest reputations in the city for being a hoe. So when I heard her name, I just knew that he fucked because he was drunk as fuck and couldn't see straight. I know she hopped on his dick without hesitation. All he really says is, she's a cool as chick and if people stop judging her on her looks and the fact that she likes to fuck, they would see her as a cool ass woman too. He asking way too fucking much.

I don't give two fucks about what he trying to prove when it comes to this chick. She big, black and she a hoe; a big time hoe at that. Why the fuck would I want his mouth on me after he at some point had his mouth on her? Just thinking about the shit is about to make me sick to the fucking stomach. Do I hate that I let Demetrius get to me. Yes. And I would never let that shit happen again.

I know I'm a fine ass woman. I have options, men and women. Sometimes I stick my toe in the lady pond, so I shouldn't be tripping over anything when it comes to Demetrius. What I should've done was change my damn number. So when he called, I wouldn't answer. After a while, he got the picture and stopped calling, until now.

As I sat in my living room on this hot, sunny, summer afternoon I thought about texting him real quick and sending him a fucked up message. After thinking on it, he might like it.

I heard the noise of kids playing and music blasting outside. Sitting on the sofa, I turned to look out the window. My sofa sat directly in front of it. The block was full of neighbors. I could've went out and engaged or I could've even called up my girls and hung out. But the truth of the matter is, Demetrius ass is on my mind.

Thinking back to the day I met his sorry ass almost makes me want to cry. I saw him with another female and me being who I am, when he gave me that eye after they both came out of the Popeye's, I returned the same look. It wasn't long after that, maybe a week that I saw him again at a friend's house. It was Friday and according to my friend Nikki, it was fish fry day. Whenever this day came around I was sure to be in the house.

Demetrius was friends with Nikki's sometime boo Jerald, who only came around to fuck or make her life miserable with all his baby momma drama. Little did I now that I would be fucking with Jerald later on down the road. We'll get to that a little later, but right now, back to when I first saw Demetrius. I immediately knew who he was and I liked what I was seeing. Tall, athletic build and a set of gorgeous white teeth. When he smiled it was like someone had painted a white line on a chocolate canvas.

You can tell he thought he was GOD'S gift to the ladies, just by how he would place his hands on the small of their back as he moved through the crowd to say hi to everyone. The women from what I could tell were all giggles. Nikki must've seen me watching him because she damn sure came over to me to stop my stare.

"Girl don't fuck with that. I've heard that man will have you sucking your thumb and calling him daddy."

"Nikki get the fuck out of here. You acting like you're forgetting who the fuck I am. I'm Shane and I don't let any man get under my skin. Hell, it's too many out her for that shit."

"Shane or no Shane, I'm trying to warn you. You can ask any woman in here that wasn't smiling when he came in the room; I guarantee he had something to do with their unhappiness."

Nikki and her big booty walked back into the cramped kitchen. As of a matter of fact, her entire apartment was small. You could put twenty people in it comfortably but her shin digs always had fifty plus people. The back door was open, front door was open and the fans were going. Drinks in either a red or blue cup were in the majority of people's hands and the music was loud; but on point.

As I was about to go the makeshift bar and pour me a drink, I saw a pretty young woman standing up against a wall talking to Jerald. They look like they had history. The way he was all up on her as if his woman wasn't in the kitchen. I don't know what they were talking about but all that shit changed when she saw the guy I was trying to holla at, walk through the door. She said something to Jerald, he turned to look towards the door, waved his hand in that direction and walked away.

I don't know who the girl is but I watched her watch him, which made me watch the both of them. The other girl whom I didn't know and I were almost right across from one another when he walked in our direction. Just by her body language and smile I knew he was about to go over to her, but he didn't.

"What are the odds of us running into each other here?" Demetrius asked.

The Demon Within | Jamee

I was still shocked that he walked over.

"Not that small considering this is Chicago and regardless of what people say, it's not that big. You're bound to run into a few people you've seen here or there." I swirled my drink in my cup and gave a half smile.

"Well, I guess you're right. If you didn't have a drink I would of asked could I make you one. So my next question would be, are you here with your man?"

I knew that was his code to let me know whether I had a man or not, we could still do whatever came to mind.

"Last I checked you were the one walking out of Popeye's with a woman, not me. So I guess my question to you would be, where's your woman tonight?"

He smiled and slid right on pass me to fix him a drink before speaking.

"First off, she's not my woman. Second, I'm very much single so it's perfectly fine that we mingle."

"Cute, don't quit your day job. Whether you know it or not, that woman across the way has been staring at us the whole time you walked over here. I don't know you but I will fuck a bitch up if she on some goofy shit."

He didn't even cut his eyes in her direction.

"Oh, that's a good friend of mine that's all."

He turned and raised his glass to her, then she walked towards the kitchen mean mugging.

"Some friend. Does she have a name? Just in case I meet her on the street and things get ugly."

"Stop, things won't get ugly. She's harmless and her name is Storry."

It's funny how as time went on we became really good friends, without her knowing that I too was sleeping with Demetrius.

We continued to talk and decided that we would hook up that night. He did tell me that he wasn't looking for a woman and that he didn't want a commitment. Hell, I was cool with that. I didn't want a man either but I gathered that's just what he was saying not to look eager. Hell, why would I want one when there are so many to choose from.

The same girl that was eyeballing us so hard finally made her way over to Demetrius that night, it didn't bother me one damn bit. She was rubbing all over him and he let her. He would whisper something in her ear and she would giggle, this shit went on for a few minutes. I actually found it to be pathetic…on her part.

Once some days went by, I actually got a call from Demetrius; I almost forgot that I had given him my number. We talked late at night. Mostly about the work that he does and how no matter what, he does not and I repeat does not want a woman. Any man that keep saying he doesn't want a woman is the kind of man that's out here fucking many women. He just doesn't want to have to answer for any of his wrong doings.

Our conversation continued smoothly. Especially when the topic of me and him slapping bellies came up; I was totally down for it. Truth be known, I was down for it the night we met. I really wanted to bring up the woman who was all on his nut sack that night but since he didn't bring her up neither would I. There was no need to talk about her anyway. That night, I enjoyed getting to know him.

We finally got together the day after our conversation. In my mind, I was ready to take him places he had never seen before, but before I could show any of that he showed me that he was the king in bed.

There was nothing romantic about meeting him, there was no flowers or soft music playing in the back ground. The only thing that was apparent was that he had drinks and weed on deck. The music was from his phone, he had blue toothed to his speakers. I knew right there and then that we were going to have a wham bam thank you ma'am kind of session...boy was I wrong.

Once he offered me drinks and some smoke, shit I was on cloud nine. A couple of hours went by that night before we even made any reference to sex. He was feeling good and I was feeling good. He didn't make one move so after three glasses of 1800 and two blunts I could've fell on my face and not felt anything. I was feeling very frisky and he was sitting at the wooden table in the dining room in a wooden chair. I was glad I had on an all-purpose dress because he was about to smoke another blunt; until I straddled him. Once I straddled him and began kissing him, he took the lead by rubbing and caressing every inch of my body. His large hands manhandled me by grabbing me around my throat and requesting that I fuck him now.

I did as I was told. His third leg felt good and full under me, and I was ready to ride the rodeo at that moment. I reached under myself and slid him inside of me. I was already slick with my own juices so penetration was easy. He filled every inch of me. I squeezed my muscles and started rocking back and forth; I was able to bounce on his dick as well, thanks to me wearing wedges that night. He pulled my dress down in front and let my breast fall out, as he sucked and nibbled on my nipples. I continued to moan out and fuck him more aggressively.

This went on all night, well into the next morning. I was flipped upside down for oral sex, my knees were at my damn ears, there wasn't a place on my body that his dick didn't enter, and I loved every minute of it. At one point I wanted to scream out and cry my orgasm were so damn hard, I felt light headed. That's something I had never had done to me and at that point for about six months we had sex frequently. And like a fucking fool, I feel in love with

Demetrius.

Jerald

I was heading over to Tessa's house to see what kind of agreement we could come to regarding the twins. I feel at this point in my life that I can now provide a place for them as well. They don't have to stay with me but I do want a real shared custody of our children. She says that she's trying to get her shit together and I want to her to get her shit together. I don't want the mother of my children out her fucked up off that damn liquor or still hopping from dick to dick. She did say they could stay with me during the summer but I want this to extend past the summer.

I know her self-esteem is low but damn. I never seen a woman fuck so many. It's not like she's a nympho, she doing the shit so she won't be alone, and that's fucked up in itself. I knew this about her before she even told me. It's one thing I can say about Tessa, she doesn't hold anything back from me. She usually tells me about the men that she's taken down. I guess she feels like I'm that one person that she could talk to about anything; not to mention, she really does want me back. Wait! She never had me, we were never a couple, we smashed a few times and she ended up pregnant.

If it wasn't for Shane, maybe I would try something with Tessa. But dammit, I refuse to smell the scent of another man's dick between her legs all the time. Not saying that Shane's perfect but I don't have to worry about her being a hoe out here in these streets. Now don't get me wrong, I still do me from time to time, especially in the last couple of days since Shane's been acting weird and shit. She acts like she doesn't want to talk about whatever is bothering her and I don't feel like getting into it either.

I walked out on my stoop and just took in the morning summer air. I had my phone in hand ready to call Tessa. I looked at my phone and saw that Shane was calling me, I felt petty because I didn't answer her. I didn't really have anything to say at this point, I wanted her to figure her shit out and I had some family shit to deal with my damn self. After Shane was off the line I called Tessa. She must've had her phone in her hand because after one ring she answered immediately.

"What's good Jerald?"

"Nothing much. Sitting out on the stoop enjoying the sun and air this morning."

"What you doing this morning?"

"Well, this is Saturday so the twins are sitting in front of the television laughing at cartoons and eating cereal. As for me, I'm about to straighten up the house and prepare tacos for later. I know you had to work different hours last week, so are you coming back to get them or was all that shit you were talking gone out the window?"

"I wanted to come over and talk to you if that's cool and yes they are coming back."

"Of course it's cool. When you're ready to come over just come. We'll be here."

After our conversation I didn't even call Shane ass back. I went inside and got myself ready to go see my kids and Tessa. I wasn't sure how this was going to turn out. She's always sure that I want to take the kids from her and that's never been the case. I just want to be a part of their lives and not just when she wants me to.

Getting ready to walk to Tessa's front door and my phone starts ringing again and yes, it's Shane again. I'm definitely not going to answer now that I'm on my way to see the kids. I'll get back at her ass once I'm done handling this business.

I rang the doorbell and when Tessa opened the door I was shocked. She didn't have her normal booty shorts on and damn near transparent shirts on. She did have on some black capris and a pink tank top and she had on a bra. She must be changing because I don't think I've ever seen her without something on that exposed some part of her body.

"Hey Jerald, good to see you."

I heard the words come out of her mouth. When I looked up, she was back over at the counter top sitting on one of the bar stools.

"Good to see you too Tessa. I must say this is a change and it's not a change that I'm use to. I must say though, it's a good change."

Tessa looked down at her new look and was pleased that I liked it.

"I'm glad that you approve of it. If I'm going to do right, I just can't stop drinking and smashing dudes randomly I might add. I have to change everything about me. Oh and before I go any further, guess who the fuck is in town?"

"Who?"

"Demetrius ass. He stopped by and said he'll be here for another day or two. He said he was going to hit you up."

"Damn, my boy back in town! That's what's up. I'll hit him later. And as for you, I guess it's safe to say that he came to see you for more than a hug."

I threw that in there because like I said, Tessa hops from dick to dick. Actually, she didn't know we were friends when she started sleeping with him, so I can't be mad he her.

"Well, you know how I do. Like I told you years ago before I had the twins when you came to me and told me that you smashed Storry's ass, I was pissed. She knew how I felt about you and how I've felt for years. No matter how hard I act I still feel this way, it's no secret. Storry acts as if she can have any man she wants, when she wants. To make it be known she fucked you. It became my business to seek out the men that she's crazy for and fuck them repeatedly. When she think she got it like that, I'll be standing in the back ground saying; nope, no you don't."

"Damn, Tessa, you're a cold piece of work and I've apologized to you many times for sleeping with Storry. It only happened twice to be exact."

"It wasn't that good-"

Damn, Tessa cut my ass off because I guess I've told this story a number of times.

"Look, you had some of Storry's pussy. I wasn't in it. If it wasn't good, so what. If it was good, still so what. Pussy is made to make a man bust and if you busted a nut then it was good…enough."

I already knew this shit was going to go left but fuck it I'm here. If this must be talked about then so be it.

"Why do you have to cut me off like that? I let you talk when you have something to say so let me do the same."

Tessa looked at me like she really would rather be doing anything else but having this conversation.

"I've never said shit about you fucking Demetrius or Cornelius but you damn sure won't let Storry go."

"Yes. I fucked them only because she fucked you after knowing how I felt about you and hell, at the time I had no idea that these were your boys. It was all about getting Storry back, it had nothing to do with you."

I was done with this merry-go-round like I said before. She dick hops and that's not what I want in my life. Should I be mad that she smashed two homies, yes. Am I mad, no.

"Look, Tessa, I came over here to talk about the kids not who fucked who, when and whether a nut was busted or not."

There was some silence so I took this time to go over and talk and play with the kids while Tessa sat over there pouring her another drink. Damn near an hour went pass before we finally spoke. Mainly about what I intended to come over here and talk about in the beginning. I expressed how I wanted us to share custody of the kids and how I didn't want to be in their lives only when she would call.

She actually agreed, and I was elated. I know the subject of the kids is touchy with her, especially since the kids are very much her everything; without them she would crumble and die. By her agreeing, I know that she needs help or just some time away for herself. She did ask did I see a real relationship between us and honestly, I didn't know what to say.

Tessa

It's been a week since Jerald brought his ass over here and drummed up bad memories for me. I know men don't give two shits about getting pussy even if it's from a woman that's your best friend. It's just pussy to them. Well I'm here to tell all men that it's not just some pussy; pussy has names and attachments to them that could fuck up any relationship. Lucky for Jerald we were not in a relationship and Storry broke sister code. For that, I'm going to keep smashing Demetrius and Cornelius until I'm ready to stop, especially Demetrius ass.

I don't make fuss about the men I sleep with. Yeah some are homies, that's not my concern. Even if I had known that I was sleeping with Jerald's homies, I still wouldn't have stopped.

Like I told him, this was bigger than him. As much as I thought that Storry was my true friend I came to find out that she treats me like the rest behind my back. If she doesn't think Cornelius, Demetrius and Jerald have told me some foul shit, she's sadly mistaken.

Oh, believe me when I drop this little bomb on Storry she'll probably try and come for me but she ain't stupid, her bark is way bigger than her bite. I'm going to make sure that both Cornelius and Demetrius play a big part in my scheme to fuck off Storry's life, forever. I don't give two shits what's going on in their lives, this bitch Storry will not be able to talk shit behind my back and know what my kids father dick taste like; she got me all the way fucked up!

See that's what people like Storry has failed to realize. Even though I love me some dick and don't try to hide it. The men that I fuck with even when it's just sexually, confide in me like they're in confession. I can only think of it being that way because I'm not a grimy bitch, I keep secrets, I don't hold shit over people head, and

I'm honest. My life is like an open book. Yes, everyone I've slept with knows of the people I've slept with in a three month time span. I didn't have to do that. I just want everyone on the same page when fucking with me so there'll be no surprises later.

I'm not a fake bitch and I think that's one of the reasons why so many women have a problem with me. I can fuck who I want, when I want, where I want and still be respected by men. The only men that disrespect are the ones that I don't want to fuck. Men know that I keep it one hundred with them. There's no guessing game when it comes to me, so that takes away all of that playing shit that these women play.

Including Storry ass, even though Cornelius and Demetrius are friends they don't know shit about each other fucking her. I bet they don't know Jerald has smashed too. But it's very convenient for her to drag my name through shit and make herself look better. Let's just see how well she holds her shit together after she finds out that

they know each other, and me.

Storry

I don't know what the fuck is going on in my life. This last month has been emotional as hell and I'm ready to get off this boat and hop on a new one. For the life of me, I can't figure out why the fuck Cornelius keep putting his fucking hands on me. Not to mention, I've already had to visit the hospital for bruised ribs. I don't know why he do the things he do and all I try to do is give him chance after chance.

I'm a thick woman but I can't do shit with a man physically. I was mortified when I had to drive home naked the first time he got out of his body with me. Then I had to get out of my car with a sheet wrapped around me.

I'm just getting over my soreness from a week ago. The thought of a man putting his hand on me any harmful way is not acceptable. And no matter how much sex I give him he still on my ass.

I'm not sure what women he has dealt with over the years but I'm not the one. I really want our relationship or fuckship to be done and over with. He has called damn near every day since our last encounter and I have not answered one damn time. The only person I have told any of this too is Tessa and she didn't have the words I was looking for. She did show concern but it wasn't what I was looking for. It's almost like she didn't really care what I had gone through.

At this moment I just want to see Demetrius. He seems to make all my bad moments great again and at this point I need to feel loved. I need him in my space but he not even answering my calls. I don't even know if he's still in town. I've checked his social media pages and no activity which means, either he's still here playing with these women or he left and has gotten busy. Either way; ignoring my fucking calls is not acceptable.

I'm sitting in my living room with my feet up on the glass cocktail table watching Married to Medicine. It was On Demand. I turned my phone off because I don't want to be bothered with no one. I'm using this time to reevaluate my life and some folks are just going to have to go.

I poured me a drink and wiped away the one lonely tear that ran down my cheek. Its summer, the weather is hot and I'm in the house alone. This shit has to change.